Taking Improvement from the Assembly Line to Healthcare

The Application of Lean within the Healthcare Industry

Taking Improvement from the Assembly Line to Healthcare

The Application of Lean within the Healthcare Industry

Ronald Bercaw

CRC Press
Taylor & Francis Group
Boca Raton   London   New York

CRC Press is an imprint of the
Taylor & Francis Group, an **informa** business
A PRODUCTIVITY PRESS BOOK

CRC Press
Taylor & Francis Group
6000 Broken Sound Parkway NW, Suite 300
Boca Raton, FL 33487-2742

Printed in the United States of America on acid-free paper
Version Date: 20111003

International Standard Book Number: 978-1-4398-6239-1 (Paperback)

Library of Congress Cataloging-in-Publication Data

Bercaw, Ronald.
    Taking improvement from the assembly line to healthcare : the application of lean within the healthcare industry / Ronald Bercaw.
        p. ; cm.
    Includes bibliographical references and index.
    ISBN 978-1-4398-6239-1 (pbk. : alk. paper)
    I. Title.
    [DNLM: 1. Health Care Sector--organization & administration. 2. Delivery of Health Care--organization & administration. 3. Efficiency, Organizational. 4. Organizational Innovation--economics. 5. Quality Improvement--standards. W 74.1]

LC Classification not assigned
362.1068--dc23   2011038264

Visit the Taylor & Francis Web site at
http://www.taylorandfrancis.com

and the CRC Press Web site at
http://www.crcpress.com

Contents

Acknowledgments

There are many people and organizations and one deity to thank for their contributions in creating this book.

A special thanks to the many healthcare organizations that allowed me the precious gift of working with them to achieve improvement. I assure you I have learned as much from you as you have from me.

To Lynn Harrison, Heather Wood, and Mike de Graauw who all provided valuable feedback on parts of the manuscript.

To Jerry and Al, who as my Sensei provided me the core knowledge about Lean improvement. I will always be grateful.

To Mike D., Scott, Heidi, Bob, Laurie, Mike E., and Steve: Collectively you make up some of the great Lean minds of this century. The world is a better place with all of you in it.

To Heather, Derrick, Ashley, Michael, and Ryan: You had to deal with my absences far more than anyone ever imagined. I love you all!

Finally to Tami, none of this work would be possible without your love, guidance, and understanding. For countless small reasons and several larger ones, this woman leaves me in awe and in love.

Introduction

After having worked in management in industrial operations for a decade, I found myself promoted into a new position as site manager. In this role, I had operating responsibilities for everything in the local organization except sales. The plant was a corporate acquisition from a private owner completed about three years earlier. We had the right things in place to be successful.

The market had been growing by greater than 10% yearly. The plant was filled with many experienced, 20+ year employees with all kinds of technical experience. Product engineering had the latest technology in design software, and a team was motivated to deliver. The corporation had capital to support any investment we needed, and we had a North American sales force with penetration into every major market. We had just completed a new IT system start-up and had the latest enterprise software to link our plants, sales, and corporate offices together. Despite these advantages, we were hemorrhaging losses. The plant had made no money in the three years since the acquisition. It was my job to bring my operations expertise to this facility and convert it to a profitable contributor to the organization.

In my third week, near the end of January 1998, we faced a "special visit." The CEO of the corporation, the CEO of the division, and all the division vice presidents were coming to the plant for a tour and division board meeting. We completed all the necessary steps in anticipation of the visit. First, we cleaned the place from pillar to post. This was no small feat as we had inventory everywhere. Then we organized round-robin presentations by department heads to update the status in their respective areas of responsibility. Finally, we choreographed the plant tour. We identified speakers and scripted the key points for discussion. Everything went off without a hitch. Until I was asked for an executive summary of what it would take to make the plant profitable. As I stammered through the obligatory, "I've only been here a few weeks" line, I gave a few of my early impressions on areas of focus for the next 90 to 180 days. As a whole, my comments were pretty lame.

The day closed with comments from the corporate CEO. "We've been trying for three years to get this plant profitable; I'll allow one more year to get the ship turned." I'll never forget those words, "You have one more year." Aside from the fact that I had just bought a new home, I hadn't sold my current home; even worse, I hadn't even relocated my family yet! What would I tell the staff associates in the plant? They had their lives and their families tied to the success of the plant as well. Nearly 500 lives would be affected by the plant's success or failure, and a failure would exert negative impacts on the supply base and community. Well, we had a year. I hoped it was enough.

It was time to get to work. I did all the traditional things that I learned earlier in my career. We had to cut costs, reduce lead times on products, and dramatically improve our quality. Fortunately, we didn't have to worry about sales! In no particular order, over the next six months, we executed the following:

■ Turned over ~50% of the management personnel. The fastest way to change the people was to change the people.
■ We consolidated all raw materials to a single vendor. Bidding the group of materials allowed us a favorable purchase price variance.
■ Cut all discretionary spending: office supplies, coffee, magazine subscriptions, bottled water.
■ Put a freeze on capital spending. Depreciation was only running about 5 to 6% of sales, but we needed every percentage on the income statement.
■ Implemented work center productivity measurements. We needed work center standards and accountability.
■ Improved the costing accuracy of the engineering team to better match actual production.
■ Initiated ISO 9001 certification at the division level, hoping this would improve our quality.

As we made changes, sales continued to increase. The margin line moved a bit and the machine centers performed better under a standard cost system, but the profit and loss statement was still dismal. On the balance sheet, despite the growth in sales, our annualized inventory turns plummeted to about 5%. We had six months to go and I was out of bullets. I didn't know what else I could do to improve the performance of the facility. We needed a miracle.

Call it fate, call it dumb luck; Miracle 1 arrived in the form of a mass mailing—a conference flyer. After reviewing the flyer, I proclaimed, "That's exactly what we need. Where do I get this lightning in a bottle?" "Apply the Toyota Production System" to your organization read the flyer and

■ Reduce lead-times by up to 80%
■ Improve productivity by 25%
■ Reduce inventory by 50%
■ Reduce defects by 75%

There was a small problem, however. We had no money to send someone to the conference but the seed was planted and I went to work to find someone who could help. Miracle 2 arrived. I was introduced to Jerry McCormick, principal of J.D. McCormick and Associates. Jerry had recently retired as the vice president of operations at Milwaukee Electric Tool and started a consulting practice based on the application of Lean principles to cellular manufacturing. Before working with Milwaukee Electric Tool, Jerry had a very successful career with Vickers Hydraulics in Arkansas. He was and remains the epitome of a southern gentleman and an outstanding operations expert.

Shortly after our initial phone call, Jerry visited our facility. We walked through the operation and Jerry asked a lot of questions. What types of products do you make? What types of volumes do you produce? How many employees do you have? What markets do you serve? What is your cost structure? Many of the questions were typical for purposes of assessing a business.

At the end of the tour, I asked Jerry what he thought of our operation. He responded with a smile, "I think you have done a nice job with a batch operation." I had no idea what that meant at the time, but looking back his comment was very gracious. In Lean terms, you will frequently here about a batch or traditional operation versus a Lean operation. Most of us have learned and continue to learn about traditional operations, with optimization of machine and work centers reinforced with standard cost systems that encourage "wasteful" operations. We'll discuss the comparison of traditional versus Lean operations in more detail in Chapters 2 and 3. What I want to highlight here is that I spent more than a decade learning and mastering a system that was antiquated, ineffective, expensive, wasteful, and delivered poor quality. *The first lesson to learn when embarking on a Lean journey is that the principles, applications, and techniques of Lean go against everything that you have spent years trying to master.*

This makes the learning curve very steep because you need to accomplish two tasks to be successful. First, you must learn and understand the "new" way of doing things. Second, you must unlearn the old ways of doing things. As you ponder that concept for a moment, I suggest a bit of self reflection. How often in your career or life have you had the opportunity to unlearn something? To be great in a Lean organization, you must apply the principles of improvement to everything your organization does. If we had time to think about problems and issues, that might not be too difficult, but we are bombarded every day with issues, questions, and challenges. Our past training and experience guide us to think in a certain way. In the heat of the moment, we always rely on our strengths that are aligned with our traditional training and experiences. We'll discuss some approaches to help guide our thinking and break this habit in Chapter 3.

After hiring Jerry, we went right to work. The physical changes happened so fast, it is difficult to recall the discrete steps. At a high level, the following actions were completed:

- The facility was reorganized into six cells: three based on product family, one shipping cell, one engineering cell, and one customer service cell.
- Ninety percent of indirect labor was reallocated directly to cells. The functions that remained centralized included planning, human resources, and accounting. Departments dissolved included maintenance, scheduling, receiving, quality, and material handling (accounting and sales were corporate functions).
- The entire facility was trained in Lean principles.
- The entire facility implemented a 5S system.
- All scheduling and materials management were placed on a pull system resulting in a 200% increase in inventory turns.
- One item flow covering standard work, balanced work, operational methods sheets, visual management, and process control was implemented over a 90-day period. This changed the profitability of the operation from negative to positive.
- We developed a cross-trained flexible workforce and tied wages to an individual's ability to demonstrate proficiency in multiple jobs and implemented a profit sharing incentive.
- Indirect labor cost was reduced about a third within two years.
- Engineering prototype development was reduced from 17 days to about 3.
- Square footage requirements for the facility shrunk from 140,000 to less than 90,000.
- Sales grew ~50% over a three-year period.
- We realized that with all this improvement, we had a long, long way to go.

The evolution of this plant was the most rewarding activity of my career to that date, and I became a life-long disciple of Lean improvement. The actions that unfolded created opportunities for many people; 140 jobs were saved, impacting 500 people when you count families. Tax money was provided to the community. Customer needs were satisfied, and we were rewarded with growth of sales and profits. Everyone shared in bonus opportunities. Members of my staff were promoted across the organization because of their Lean knowledge and ability to apply it to produce results.

Over the next 10 years, I was blessed with the opportunity to apply Lean principles to electronic power reliability systems, test and measurement equipment, a wide variety of U.S. Navy, Army, and Air Force maintenance applications, U.S. Pentagon business systems, carpet backing, furniture, retail and distribution, and both U.S. and Canadian healthcare systems. What I have learned over this time is that the principles of improvement are universal. They can be applied in any industry. Factors such as union or non-union status, public or private organization, shop floor or administration level, local or international operation, manufacturing or engineering methods, simple or complex systems, small or large size, horizontal, vertical, or no integration, highly leveraged or limited IT capability do not matter. If work is done, "waste" is present. If waste is present, improvement can occur through the application of Lean principles.

This book is about the application of Lean in healthcare. The lessons about embracing improvement as a strategy began 60 years ago on a factory assembly line and eventually moved to programs within our current complex medical environment. We begin with a call to action. The healthcare system faces a storm composed of high cost, the stress caused by an aging population, and a shortage of talent that imposes new demands never seen before on our communities, our states or provinces, and even our countries.

Learning some tools and results obtained from these tools is not sufficient. The first chapter focuses on how to get started on your own improvement journey. We'll cover the necessary steps to determine the outcomes desired, select the areas of focus, deliver the improvement, sustain the results, and then spread the progress to other areas. This chapter is followed by reviewing critical success factors. The lessons learned can be shared to help mitigate project risk and shorten the learning curve for your organization. Chapter 3 presents an overview of the tools used in the healthcare setting to help us "see and eliminate" waste. After some discussion of tools, we use case studies to illustrate how the application of the tools in healthcare led to world class rates of improvement in the areas of emergency medicine, diagnostic imaging, orthopedic clinics, general internal medicine, administration, and finally community care. We conclude with the leadership challenges your organization must address to get to the tipping point—the place where the culture of your organization is changed and can deliver continuous improvement in clinical quality and patient safety, lead time and/or access, productivity and/or cost, and staff development and/or engagement.

Those who work in the healthcare field today receive the greatest gift anyone can ever receive: the ability to serve mankind and make the world a better place. Because of your calling, you are in a position to receive this gift *every* day. I am hopeful that this book, in some small way, can help you take even better advantage of your gift.

Author

Ronald Bercaw is the president of Breakthrough Horizons, LTD, a management consulting company specializing in world class improvement through the application of the Toyota Production System, more commonly known as "Lean." With over 20 years of experience in operations, his Lean management experience was gained through multiple enterprise transformations in different industries including custom packaging, power reliability electronics assembly, and test and measurement products.

Educated at Purdue University, Ron learned the details and disciplined applications of Lean principles, habits, and tools from both the Shingijutsu Sensei and their first generation disciples. Working in both shop floor and above-the-shop-floor areas, Ron has vigorously strived to remove waste from businesses through the involvement and ideas of the people doing the work.

Ron has consulting experience in the healthcare sector (U.S. and Canadian health systems including primary care, acute care, and community applications of both clinical and back shop improvement), the commercial sector (administration, manufacturing, distribution, supply chain, and engineering), and the public sector (U.S. Army, U.S. Navy, U.S. Air Force including MRO, Pentagon, and Surgeon General Assignments).

Chapter 1

Critical Condition: Why Change Is Needed Now

Introduction: The Perfect Storm

Quality healthcare is a cornerstone of any healthy society. In North America, we have access to sophisticated medical technology, world renowned physicians, highly trained nurses and hospital personnel, advanced pharmaceuticals, and innovations in diagnosis and treatment. But for all our sophistication, serious problems afflict healthcare systems across North America today—problems that cause severe hardship for families in communities large and small.

Considering its impact on society, healthcare is arguably our most important industry. Good health is a key aspect of a productive and fulfilling life no matter what a person's age, cultural background, social status, or career. To live well and provide for ourselves and others, we all depend on a strong healthcare system that can help us prevent illness and access effective treatment when we need it. Needless to say, building and maintaining that robust healthcare system is no easy task.

Although the healthcare systems of the United States and Canada differ significantly, a number of common challenges have emerged in both markets. Medical professionals and consumers alike are recognizing that the healthcare system is in critical condition. The situation is so serious, it requires the kind of dramatic transformation only Lean can provide.

In Canada, a publicly funded, universal access healthcare system was created in 1966. The system known as Medicare was intended to ensure that all citizens would receive the medical treatment they needed, from regular check-ups to major surgery, regardless of their ability to pay. Universal healthcare was a noble goal and the Medicare system is still a point of pride for Canadians. It's a great idea in theory. Unfortunately, it does not work well in practice. Almost a half-century after Medicare was born, Canadians are finding that their trusted healthcare system is not always there when they need it.

In an August 2010 report titled *Health Care Transformation in Canada: Change that Works, Care That Lasts*, the Canadian Medical Association (CMA) bluntly stated, "The founding principles of Medicare are not being met today either in letter or in spirit. Canadians are not receiving the value they deserve from the healthcare system."

The CMA is considered the national voice of physicians and has more than 72,000 members. In addition to advocating for public health promotion along with disease and injury prevention, the CMA seeks to provide leadership to the medical profession as the industry adapts to ongoing changes in the health-care landscape. It is a voluntary professional organization that encompasses 51 national medical organizations across all of Canada's provinces and territories.

"In both 2008 and 2009," the CMA report states, "the Euro-Canada Health Consumer Index ranked Canada 30th of 30 countries (the U.S. was not included in the sample) in terms of value for money spent on healthcare. Canadians deserve better." The report goes on to say, "Canada cannot continue on this path. The system needs to be massively transformed...." *

Coming from the nation's most prominent organization of medical professionals, the call for change could not be more urgent or clear. To be ranked 30th among 30 countries is a pretty serious shortfall—especially for a country that prides itself on universal healthcare for all! Could the situation be even worse?

To answer that, we need only look south of the border, even though the United States was not included in the 30-country study cited by the CMA. To get a perspective on how Americans feel about the healthcare they receive, let's look at recent data.

Healthcare reform in the United States has been the subject of intense political debate and public concern for decades. Apart from the quality of healthcare service, the issue in the United States is access. In 2007, the U.S. Census Bureau reported that 15.7% of the population, or 45.7 million people, had no health insurance whatsoever.† Not surprisingly, the majority of personal bankruptcies in

---

* Canadian Medical Association. 2010. Health Care Transformation in Canada: Change That Works, Care That Lasts. Ottawa.
† U.S. Census Bureau. 2008. Income, Poverty, and Health Insurance Coverage in the United States, 2007. Washington, D.C.

the United States (62.1% in 2007) resulted from inability to pay medical costs.* In 2009, a Harvard study published in the *American Journal of Public Health* reported that as many as 44,789 people die each year because they have no health insurance.†

In 2000, the World Health Organization ranked the U.S. healthcare system 37th in overall performance, stuck between Costa Rica and Slovenia. (Canada was ranked 30th in that survey; France was first).‡ The average life expectancy in the U.S. is just over 78 years, which means you can expect to live longer in any other G7 country (Canada, France, Germany, Italy, Japan, or the United Kingdom).§

It's clear that in both the United States and Canada, the healthcare system is ailing…and people are suffering as a result. What are the underlying causes of these depressing statistics? In fact, four distinct factors are combining to create the "perfect storm" now damaging North American healthcare. To heal our hospitals and clinics and start receiving the medical care we deserve, we need a prescription that provides:

1. Improved quality of care
2. Increased access to services
3. Affordable cost
4. Improved resource utilization to address labor shortfalls

Without transformation in all four areas, the North American healthcare system is likely to remain critically ill—and take hardworking Canadians and Americans down with it. Fortunately, by applying Lean principles and techniques, there's hope that healthcare can make a complete recovery. Before we embark on the treatment, let's look closely at the four areas where improvement is urgently needed.

Quality of Care

According to the 2008 National Healthcare Quality Report (an annual report commissioned by the U.S. Congress to track healthcare performance), patients

---

* Himmelstein, D.J. et al. August 2009. Medical bankruptcy in the United States, 2007: Results of a national study. *American Journal of Medicine,* 122 (8), 1–3.
† December 2009. *American Journal of Public Health,* 99 (12), 6.
‡ World Health Organization. 2000. *World Health Organization assesses the world's health system.* Press release 4421, Geneva.
§ United Nations. 2006. World Population Prospects: Table A.17 [1], Life expectancy at birth (years) 2005–2010. New York.

in the U.S. received recommended care less than 60% of the time.* The results of those discrepancies may be very serious. According to a report titled *To Err is Human* from the Institute of Medicine, a Massachusetts-based organization dedicated to healthcare improvement, between 44,000 and 98,000 deaths per year occur in U.S. hospitals from what are called "adverse events." In other words, errors in hospitals caused more annual deaths than car accidents, breast cancer, or AIDS. (Significantly, the Institute for Healthcare Improvement says in its report that "safety breakthroughs are achievable by adapting solutions from outside healthcare… [including] 'Lean production.'") Of course, mistakes are made in hospitals all over the world. In Canada, a 2000 study found that 7.5% of patients admitted to Canadian hospitals experienced one or more adverse events and that more than one-third (36.9%) of the incidents were judged "highly preventable."[†]

The errors were not caused by uncaring or incompetent individuals; they were caused by process. Every day in hospitals across North America, you can see heartbreaking evidence of the failures of process—and you don't have to go into patients' rooms to find it. The evidence is in plain view, starting in hospital corridors.

The corridor is where 70-year old Verne Sadoway ended up when he urgently needed surgery to remove a blockage in his prostate. Lying in the hallway of a hospital in British Columbia's Okanagan Valley, he felt invisible, had no privacy, and was constantly bothered by lights and noise. "After the third night, I said, 'I've got to get out of here; I've got to get some sleep.'"[‡]

Sadoway's experience might have been humiliating and uncomfortable, but at least it was not fatal. In September 2008, Brian Sinclair died in an emergency department waiting room in Winnipeg, Manitoba. Sinclair, a double amputee with a speech impediment, checked in with personnel at the triage desk and then sat in his wheelchair in the waiting room—for 34 hours! Another person in the waiting room brought his death to the attention of hospital staff. An autopsy showed that he died of a treatable blood infection.

Access to Services

In both Canada and the United States, consumers have come to expect long waits for emergency services. In 2009, the average length of stay in a U.S. emergency

---

* Institute of Medicine of the National Academies. April 2010. Future Directions for the National Healthcare Quality and Disparities Reports: Report Brief, Washington, D.C.
† Canadian Medical Association. 2004. The Canadian Adverse Events Study: The Incidence of Adverse Events Among Hospital Patients in Canada. Ottawa.
‡ Priest, Lisa. Bed Shortage so Severe it's 'Appalling.' *The Globe and Mail*. November 5, 2008. Toronto.

department rose to 4 hours, 7 minutes—up slightly from 2008.* While that time is far more manageable than the 34-hour horror story above, more than 4 hours is still an excruciatingly long time to sit in a waiting room when you or a loved one are injured or in pain.

According to the Canadian Association of Emergency Physicians, writing in 2005, "Hospital and bed closures, coupled with an aging and increasingly complex patient population, have created an overcrowding crisis in emergency departments across the country." In the year the report was written, Canadian hospital bed occupancy was about 95%.† Although more recent national figures are not available, in 2010 the Horizon Health Network in New Brunswick reported several local hospitals operating above that capacity figure, with the Upper River Valley Hospital at 107.8% capacity. Dean Cummings, executive director of that hospital, explains that when beds for admitted patients are insufficient, "what happens is they're basically admitted and held in the ER until a bed opens up on the floor." Of course, for all the justifiable concern over emergency department overcrowding, it represents just a small part of the picture of overall access to healthcare services.

The complex issues of access and waiting times have been priorities for Canadian policymakers since 2004, when national benchmarks were established to make waiting times for medical procedures consistent and appropriate across the country. Five priority areas were identified for benchmarking and ongoing tracking: joint replacement (hip and knee); sight restoration (cataract surgery); heart (coronary artery bypass graft [CABG]), surgery; diagnostic imaging (magnetic resonance imaging [MRI] and computed tomography [CT]), and cancer care (radiotherapy). Although the initiative marks a step forward, analysts admit that true improvement is still some distance away.

The Wait Time Alliance (WTA) for Timely Access to Health Care is a group of doctors and medical professionals who share concern about delayed access to care for their patients and work collaboratively with stakeholders to improve wait times. According to the WTA's most recent report, "Despite some improvement in wait time grades, long waits for care continue to be an issue and much of the wait time picture remains clouded in mystery." Furthermore, "One difficulty in providing a true picture...is that most current wait time reporting focuses only on the five priority areas, a far cry from the hundreds of different types of care offered in physicians' offices, hospitals, and other settings across the country each day."

---

* Pulse Report 2010: Emergency Department. Inpatient Perspectives on American Health Care. Press Ganey. http://www.pressganey.com/researchResources/hospitals/pulseReports.aspx
† Canadian Association of Emergency Physicians. June 16, 2005. Taking Action on the Issue of Overcrowding in Canada's Emergency Departments. Ottawa.

The report goes on to examine the process of reporting on wait times, saying that measurement starts "from a specialist physician's decision to treat a patient to the time the patient receives treatment." As well, "Patients can face long waits from family physician/general practitioner (GP) referral to specialist consultation or multiple waits for several tests and procedures associated with a single care pathway."[*]

The government-established benchmarks for wait times are: 26 weeks for hip and knee replacement, 16 weeks for cataract surgery, 28 days for cancer treatment, and 26 weeks for cardiac bypass surgery. No national benchmarks have yet been established for diagnostic imaging. Benchmark maximum wait times for emergency departments are currently between 4 and 6 hours. But benchmarks and statistics aside, any wait seems far too long when dealing with a serious illness. The time between diagnosis and treatment can seem endless. A 3-week wait for cancer treatment, for example, can feel like an eternity.

According to a 2008 Ipsos-Reid poll, 41% of Canadians said they had to wait longer than they thought was reasonable to gain access to a specialist, while 30% said they had to wait too long for surgery or other medical treatment. Over a third (35%) said they or members of their households had to wait longer than they thought they should to see a family physician. Meanwhile, according to the College of Family Physicians of Canada, millions of Canadians (about 5 million in 2006) or 17% of the population do not have their own family doctors, making them all the more dependent on walk-in clinics and emergency departments.

In the United States, the Centers for Disease Control and Prevention report that visits to emergency departments (EDs) are up 23% in the last decade. Of the 117 million ED visits in 2007, only about one-quarter were covered by Medicaid or the State Children's Health Insurance Program. Over the same period (2000 to 2008), the number of Americans insured by their employers dropped by 3 million people.[†] According to a 2009 report by the Lewin Group (owned by United Healthcare), 86.7 million Americans were uninsured at some point in 2007 and 2008. That grim picture underlines what was widely reported after a 2007 study by *Consumer Reports*: about 40% of Americans are uninsured or underinsured—effectively stranded with no access to the health-care system.

---

[*] Wait Time Alliance. June 2010. No Time for Complacency: Report Card on Wait Times in Canada. Ottawa.

[†] Robert Wood Johnson Foundation. 2010. Barely Hanging On: Middle Class and Uninsured. Princeton, NJ.

Affordability of Healthcare Services

Considering the number of concerns about waiting times and errors, the amount of money spent for healthcare across North America may be surprising. According to the Fraser Institute (a fiscally conservative, independent think tank that promotes free market principles), healthcare spending in 2008 in Canada was predicted to be $171.9 billion or $5,170 per person, roughly 10.7% of the GDP. Among other countries that also try to provide universal access to healthcare, only Iceland and Switzerland spend more. Unfortunately, the Fraser Institute goes on to say, "Canada does not rank first in any of the seven healthcare outcome categories or in any of the comparisons of access to care, supply of technologies or supply of technicians." In the opinion of the report authors, Canada's healthcare system "produces inferior access to physicians and technology, produces longer waiting times, is less successful in preventing death from preventable causes, and costs more than any of the other systems that have comparable objectives, save the programs in Iceland and Switzerland."[*]

In Canada in 2006, per capita healthcare spending was $3,678 (U.S.). In the U.S., it was significantly higher at $6,714; the nation spent 15.3% of its GDP on healthcare, while Canada spent 10%. Interestingly, the United States spends more on healthcare per capita than any other country in the world[†] but is the only wealthy industrialized nation without some form of universal healthcare.[‡]

Where do the costs come from? Two physicians took a personal look at that question in a recent article in *MedScape Today*. Self-described "insiders" Frank J. Veith and Zvonimir Krajcer identified several hidden cost culprits. They include declining reimbursements to physicians from public insurers—a current trend that leads doctors to carry out unnecessary procedures to avoid cuts in pay, thus adding to the cost burden of the overall system.

"Physicians who do procedures are paid on the basis of the number of procedures performed," Veith and Krajcer write. "If the compensation per procedure is decreased, as is happening, the only way for a physician to maintain his or her income is to do more procedures. Accordingly, a cut in procedural reimbursement will inevitably motivate physicians to do more procedures. For reasons already mentioned, this will result in more unnecessary operations and procedures. Increased costs and unnecessary risks to patients will result."

---

[*] Fraser Institute. 2008. How Good is Canadian Health Care? Toronto.
[†] World Health Statistics, 2009. World Health Organization Press. Geneva, p. 114.
[‡] Institute of Medicine at the National Academies. 2004. Insuring America's Health: Principles and Recommendations. Washington, D.C.

These two physicians also draw important connections between the financial woes of individual hospitals, the misguided attempts to fix the problem, and the unexpected costs that result. "In one New York institution, salaried staff surgeons were ordered to increase their admissions and operations by 20% or face cuts in salary. Because most surgeons normally operate on all patients who have appropriate indications for such aggressive treatment, the only way these surgeons could possibly increase their operative load was to perform procedures that were not indicated. Such behaviors subject patients to unwarranted risks and increases costs."[*]

When you're talking about billions of dollars of healthcare spending, it may be difficult to see—as these two doctors did—that skyrocketing costs are often results of misguided processes. By applying Lean principles to the overall system, waste in the form of unnecessary spending (and unnecessary procedures) can be eliminated. As a result, the overall cost of healthcare can be reduced, making it more affordable for both consumers and public and private insurers.

Shortage of Resources

Our prescription for improving healthcare across North America also needs to address a current labor shortfall. As the population ages, more doctors and nurses will be needed. In the United States, 79 million baby boomers will soon reach old age, necessitating 200,000 more physicians by 2020. Right now, both the United States and Canada need doctors. With only 2.4 and 2.2 doctors per 1,000 people in 2005,[†] respectively, both Americans and Canadians find it harder to access doctors than their European counterparts. (Greece leads the way on the doctor-per-person score, with 4.9 physicians per thousand citizens.)

Of course, some communities have fewer doctors than others, leading to specific adverse effects on the healthcare systems in those communities. One example of an under-served community with a shortage of family doctors is Hamilton, Ontario. Although Canada has a national average of 101 family doctors per 100,000 people, Hamilton and its surrounding areas have only 76. That low number leads to a number of negative effects, one of which was highlighted in a 2010 survey by the Canadian Institute for Health Improvement (CIHI). The institute found that in Hamilton's local health integration network (encompassing a large area of Southern Ontario including 10 hospitals and more than 220,000 people over age 65), the hospitalization rate for common conditions

---

[*] Veith, F.J. and Krajcer, Z. March 2010. Why U.S. healthcare costs are out of control: two insiders' perspectives. *Medscape Today*. http://www.medscape.com/viewarticle/717542

[†] Organisation for Economic Co-operation and Development. 2007. Health Data. Paris.

such as diabetes, asthma, and high blood pressure was higher than the rates for the province of Ontario and Canada as a whole.*

In a well functioning healthcare system, these conditions are effectively managed at home under the guidance of primary care physicians. Without those physicians, people in Hamilton may not be seeking the medical advice or treatment they need—ending up with more serious conditions that require hospital care.

Doctors are not the only healthcare personnel in short supply in North America. It has been estimated that by 2025, the U.S. will face a shortage of 260,000 registered nurses—the largest shortage since the mid 1960s. The shortfall is projected despite the fact that opportunities are growing in the nursing profession faster than in other occupations. Why the shortage? Several interconnected factors are at work. Nursing school enrollment is not growing fast enough to meet demand. The thin ranks of nursing school faculty mean enrollment must be restricted. Also, the average age of RNs is increasing; more nurses are retiring as our population ages and requires more care. Add to this the stress caused by insufficient staffing and the burn-out that ensues, and the result is high turnover as many nurses exit their jobs and even leave the profession entirely.

Due to shortages of nurses, many hospital administrators encourage or require their nurses to work overtime to meet patient needs. That strategy can backfire, sometimes with tragic consequences. In 2007, the Agency for Healthcare Research and Quality found that chronic fatigue and poor sleep quality were common among healthcare workers. Sleep deprivation was likely a factor in Wisconsin in July 2006, when a veteran obstetrical nurse who had worked two eight-hour shifts back to back administered the wrong medication to a patient. When the patient died, the nurse was charged with a felony, becoming the first RN in Wisconsin to face criminal charges for a medical error.†

Tragic stories like this one remind us that every statistic about medical errors, labor shortages, budget crunches, and waiting times also extracts a human cost. Waste and inefficiency in healthcare take tolls on people both within organizations and in the communities they serve—and of course, healthcare staffers depend on hospitals for their own well-being as well as their jobs. Across North America, consumers and medical professionals alike are calling for rapid, effective change. That's our call to action. With a healthcare system in critical condition, Lean is the best possible treatment.

---

* Frketich, Joanna. May 28, 2010. Doctor shortage affects simple health. *Hamilton Spectator.* Hamilton, Ontario.

† Garrett, C. June 2008. The effect of nurse staffing patterns on medical errors and nurse burnout. *AORN Journal.* 87 (6), 1.

Chapter 2

Fundamentals of Improvement

What Is Lean?

Lean is not technically a noun. It is the adjective in "Lean thinking." It is also the title of a 1996 book by James Womack and Dan Jones that covers both the thinking and an approach that can be used by organizations to deploy the Toyota Production System.[*] Over time, the word "thinking" was no longer used and the name of the technique has shrunk simply to "Lean." Toyota Corporation, the developer of the Toyota Production System, describes its improvement strategy as "the Toyota Way"[†]—a comprehensive business approach and corresponding culture focused on continuous process improvement to deliver value to customers. Before discussing this holistic approach toward improvement, it is helpful to have a basic understanding of improvement terminology.

Value-Added Activities

Lean improvement is based on two themes: (1) continuous improvement (a different name for elimination of waste), and (2) respect for people. Figure 2.1 illustrates these themes. Elimination of waste means the reduction of

---

[*] Womack, J. and Jones, D. 1996. Preface. *Lean Thinking*. Simon & Schuster, New York, p. 12.
[†] Liker, J. 2004. Foreword. *The Toyota Way*. McGraw Hill, New York, p. xi.

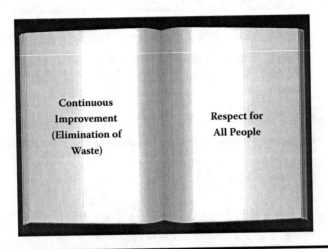

Figure 2.1   Themes of Lean improvement.

non-value-added activity. To understand the first theme of elimination of waste, it is essential to understand the value-added and non-value-added principles. Every activity that occurs in an organization falls into one of two categories: value-added or non-value-added. A value-added activity during production is an easy concept to grasp. Activities that change the form, fit, or function of a product are classified as value-added. Another definition of a value-added activity is any product- or service-related action for which a customer is willing to pay. Examples of value-added activities are welding and product assembly. A value-added activity for a service would be technical support service via telephone.

Non-Value-Added Activities

A non-value-added activity is by default the opposite of a value-added activity. It consumes time, space, or resources but does not change the form, fit, or function of the product. A non-value-added activity may also be defined as an activity requiring time, space, or resources for which a customer is not willing to pay. Two examples of non-value-added activity are moving a part from one machine to the next or counting inventory to ensure accuracy of on-hand quantities.

A third category involves activities required by law or business practice (for example, accreditation and third party certification). These requirements may be imposed by Occupational Safety and Health Act (OSHA) standards, ISO standards, or generally accepted accounting principles (GAAPs). While it can be tempting to classify these requirements differently, at the end of the day, they add no value for the end customer. Changing the classification of an activity does not change the value-added and non-value-added principles.

In healthcare, the definition of value is slightly different. A value-added activity *directly* meets the need of customers. To determine whether a step is value added, you must understand two issues: (1) who your customers are, and (2) what their needs are. Often in healthcare a dialogue jumps from the customer as patient and/ or caregiver to the customer as provider or administrator. Value is always specified by THE customer. There can be only one. The way I find easiest to determine the true single customer is by defining who creates the pull for the services needed. To identify the customer for a surgical procedure, we must understand where the pull for the service comes from. Since we would not need a surgical facility, sterile processing, surgical staff, surgeon, or billing department without a patient needing surgery, the patient is the customer. Value is specified by the patient, so value-added and non-value-added activities are based on the view of the patient.

The second determination is what the customer needs. Healthcare professionals often have expertise and knowledge that can be very helpful in determining customer needs. However, determining customer needs is not exclusively the role of the staff. With information available at a click of a mouse, customers (patients) are quite capable of specifying their needs. As I tell healthcare professionals, when I work with engineers designing new products, they are quick to note that consumers do not know what they want or need; thus the engineers must make those decisions for consumers since they have the technical expertise. I think everyone as a consumer can determine the features and benefits he or she seeks in a new product or service. It would be very expensive to drag an engineer around every time we shopped for a product. As consumers, we have no problem specifying value-added and non-value-added activities in our purchases. The same theory holds true for patients seeking medical services. While you may be the healthcare "engineer," the patient is generally quite capable of determining his or her needs. Your job as a service provider is to identify the activities that directly meet those needs—the value-added activities.

The following example explains the value-added and non-value-added activities involved in an ankle x-ray. We likely will need to schedule an examination date and time, register with someone when we arrive, and complete some paperwork. While all of these activities accompany a typical x-ray experience, none of them directly meets our needs so all these activities constitute non-value-added activities. To determine the value-added activity, we must identify the customer, specify his or her needs, and determine which activities directly meet those needs. The customer is the patient who needs the exam. The needs to be met include the conduct of the examination and handling of the corresponding results. The value-added activities are the actual procedure (which takes seconds), and the reading of the results (which takes minutes). But what about cleaning the table,

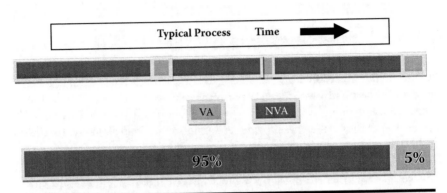

Figure 2.2 Value-added and non-value-added principles.

preparing for the examination, transcribing the results, charting the activities, and preparing and sending an invoice? These are all non-value-added activities.

The understanding of value-added (VA) and non-value-added (NVA) activities is the first lesson that must be learned to achieve improvement. The lesson is not always easy to understand. When we understand both VA and NVA activities, we can start to look at the ratio between the two activities. A typical process is 95% NVA to 5% VA. World class organizations understand this and take advantage of understanding this ratio (Figure 2.2).

Improvement using Lean fundamentals involves the identification and elimination of NVA activities. A 95% NVA level leaves a lot of room for improvement and focusing on NVA activity provides two benefits. First the improvement potential is much larger. Would you rather pay attention to the 95% opportunity or the 5% opportunity? The answer indicates why Lean organizations can show 25 to 50% improvements: they play in the 95% space. Second, the cost of improvement is significantly less. When we focus on eliminating NVA activities, we are in essence stopping some kind of work. How much does it cost to stop doing something? An NVA activity is defined as using time, space, and resources, but not directly meeting patient needs. If we eliminate NVA activities, we free up time, space, and resources and we can use them to add more value for customers!

Themes of Lean Improvement: Continuous Improvement

As noted earlier, Lean improvement is based on two themes: continuous improvement (elimination of NVA activities) and respect for people. We just spent a fair amount of time discussing VA and NVA activities. Understanding them constitutes the foundation of continuous improvement. In the simplest terms, improvement consists of seeing waste and eliminating it. The concept of improvement is sometimes referred to as *kaizen*. Kaizen is actually two words. "Kai" loosely means *change*. "Zen" means *for the better*.

The theme of continuous improvement, however, has two other tenets. Culturally, we want to create a work environment where we strive to meet targets using courage and creativity. Courage implies making individual and team decisions in the best interest of serving the customer. For example, clinic hours of operation best serve their customers from noon to 9 p.m. We have been comfortable working from 9 a.m. to 5 p.m. for years. A courageous decision would mean altering work hours in the best interest of the customer. Creativity implies using new approaches and techniques in lieu of adding resources and capital cost. Lean practitioners say, "Use creativity before capital." This implies generating solutions that take minimal resources to implement before making significant capital investments in equipment, facilities, or additional staff.

Another tenet of continuous improvement is the concept of "genchi genbutsu," loosely translated as *go to the source to find facts*. When problems arise in a workplace, how would a manager traditionally respond? Most organizations would schedule a meeting of knowledgeable experts to try to solve the problems. (To illustrate my point, if you are a manager in healthcare, I would be willing to bet that most of your time each day is spent going from one meeting to the next.) A Lean company views problems as treasures of information that show where the current process is not adequate.

A Lean manager will always go to the area where a problem occurred and observe the process to see whether the source can be identified. This is monumentally different from the traditional approach. Not going to the area where the problem occurred is the equivalent of a police detective not going to the scene of a crime to uncover forensic evidence. How effective would investigations be if the standard approach to crime solving involved scheduling a meeting at the police office and bringing in experts to solve the crime? The healthcare example I like to use is an instance where a dose of medicine was missed. This resulted in an adverse event that, while not catastrophic, warranted investigation. The question I'd like you to ponder is how many missed doses occur in conference rooms? We must go to the source to find the facts.

Themes of Lean Improvement: Respect for All People

From a global perspective, respect for all people means having a purpose for improvement. How can improvement in healthcare benefit our patients, staff,

7 Wastes

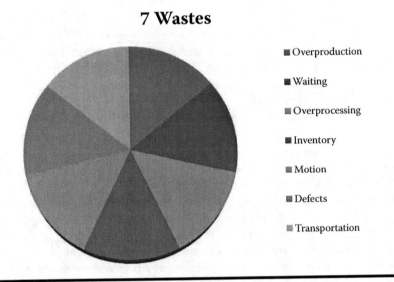

■ Overproduction

■ Waiting

■ Overprocessing

■ Inventory

■ Motion

■ Defects

■ Transportation

Figure 2.3 Seven wastes.

physicians, community agencies, and service providers? How can we improve our local community, our country, and the world as a whole? From individual and organizational perspectives, showing respect for people comes in the form of understanding them. What work do I do and what work do you do? How do we together build mutual trust? Respect is also demonstrated through individual and team responsibility. Are we doing the right thing every time? Are we following the known best way? Are we doing our best? As an organization, we want to optimize both team and individual performance. Are we sharing opportunities for personal and team development?

Seven Wastes

As we discussed earlier, NVA and waste are the same things. Over time, many different types of wastes were identified and it became possible to categorize them. The major forms found in operations became known as the seven operational wastes (Figure 2.3). Let's review all of them.

Overproduction

Overproduction is producing too much or producing too early. Let's say we mixed IV solution and we delivered a 2-day supply to a unit where a patient was recovering. At the end of the first day, the patient was discharged. The remaining (overproduced) solution would probably have been returned to the pharmacy and likely destroyed. When we overproduce, we expend labor (in this case to mix IV solutions) whose costs can never be recovered. Additionally, the disposal of the overproduced solution creates an additional and unrecoverable expense.

Waiting

Waiting causes disruptions to work flow through idle resources, stopping and starting, and time delays to customers (patients and staff). Healthcare operations commonly have to wait for service providers, diagnostics, information, equipment, and materials. Waiting is the largest single waste in healthcare. I'm sure all service providers that work in emergency departments recall occasions when patients and family members clearly expressed displeasure concerning time spent in the waiting area.

Staff members do not always see waiting as a waste. If a physical therapist walks to a patient room to provide therapy and the patient is not present, the therapist likely would not wait and would simply to go the next patient on the schedule. In this case, the therapist is not idle and adds value (provides therapy) to a different patient; the waiting was not wasteful. This argument is flawed on two fronts. First, waste was created when the therapist walked to the patient room only to find out the patient was not present. Walking to a missed appointment represents wasted motion. More importantly, waste must be viewed from the customer perspective. The therapist who does not see the missed session as wasteful is looking at the issue from the wrong pair of eyes. The patient is the customer and he or she is *waiting* for therapy.

An interesting aspect of improvement is the requirement to train yourself to see waste. Understanding the seven key wastes is a good start in learning to identify waste in your organization. Waste in healthcare is easy to spot. Look in the *waiting* room.

Overprocessing

Overprocessing is waste generated by performing work in excess of value. While this may be hard to believe, it is possible to do *more* work than the customer values. Because I travel frequently, one of my travel gadgets is a portable electronic scanner. I use it to e-mail documents related to contracts and scan receipts for expense reports. This scanner comes with software that creates expense reports, sort expenses into categories, assigns tax codes, and handles other tasks. Unfortunately, the use of the product requires many steps and work-arounds to provide the basic functions that I need. This product is over-engineered from my customer perspective; its use creates overprocessing. It is important to note, however, that other people may find these features beneficial and thus in their eyes the product does not overprocess.

As an example of overprocessing in healthcare, consider inter-professional assessment. A complex patient may be assessed by multiple nurses, physicians, and other members of an allied health team. While each team member is looking for different pieces of information to provide the best possible care, the patient may be asked the same question by two or more people. Many of you in the course of your work have heard, "I've been asked this five times already. Do you people talk to one another?" Again from the patient perspective, the healthcare organization has overprocessed. The redundancy in questioning creates work in excess of value.

Inventory

When we think of inventory, we think of supplies. All participants in a production or service environment can relate to the disruption in work when they run out of supplies. In the opposite situation, excessive supplies take up time, space, and resources but do not directly contribute to meeting customer needs.

Healthcare also involves other forms of inventory, for example, patients waiting for services. Patients may be waiting for admission, an isolation bed, test results, or other services. These patient collections represent inventory because they queue and occupy space. Perhaps a simple definition of inventory is "things" (people, items, information) waiting to be worked on. Another form of inventory is waiting in your inbox. In healthcare administration, work queues up in many areas: bills waiting to be paid, charts waiting to be coded, invoices waiting to be processed and mailed, supplies waiting to be ordered, financial reports waiting to be generated. The backlog of these items constitutes a type of inventory.

Motion

When we speak of waste of motion by staff and providers, we are talking about movement in excess of that required to create value. One form of motion is present we walk from one area to the next looking for supplies and equipment; for example, walking an extra ten steps for sanitizer because the dispenser is not located at the point of use. Sonya Pak, a quality improvement consultant with the Centre for Healthcare Quality Improvement based in Toronto tells a story of wasted motion. When she was a patient care manager in a community hospital in Ontario, her unit was running low on a form. Replenishment required the unit clerk to send a copy of the form to materials management for duplication (Figure 2.4). Sounds simple, right? Well, the process actually went like this.

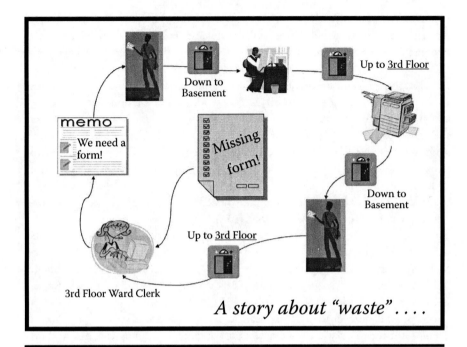

Figure 2.4   Form replenishment. (Courtesy of Sonya Pak. With permission.)

1. The unit clerk wrote a memo to materials management explaining the need for forms.
2. Materials management would request a mail pick-up from the unit to have the form delivered to its operation in the basement.
3. Upon receiving the form, the materials management associate would walk to a different floor, utilize a copy machine to make the copies, then return to material management.
4. The material management associate would then coordinate another mail pick-up and have the form supply delivered to the unit where the unit secretary would file the new supply.

I forgot to mention that the copy machine used to make the new supply was the *same* machine used by the unit that requested the copies!

Defects

Defects create waste because work is needed to correct them. Before we get too far into the waste of defects, we need to differentiate defects and errors. Work completed by humans is subject to errors. An error is a mistake in the execution of a task. An example of an error is an inadvertent failure of a physician to sign an order for a medication. Errors will be made regardless of how well-trained people are, how often they complete tasks, or how diligent and conscientious they are.

However, an error need not turn into a defect. A defect is an error that makes its way to the customer. The result is that work must be redone, corrected, or clarified. One technique for preventing errors is known as "poka-yoke," loosely translated as *mistake proofing*. The technique is cited in *Zero Quality Control*, a book by Shigeo Shingo.* While the many examples in this book appear to apply to manufacturing, the science of mistake proofing applies wherever work is done.

In healthcare, defects frequently take the form of missing information, incorrect information, or information received in an incorrect format. Defects can also be clinical: the wrong test ordered or the wrong diagnosis made. Patients can be harmed by infections acquired in hospitals or failure of a provider to follow evidence-based best practices. The Institute for Healthcare Improvement (IHI) website (www.ihi.org) contains many sources of information on improving patient safety and reducing morbidity and mortality.

As a final note on defects in healthcare, I find that a sentinel or adverse event is not the main source of a defect, although it is certainly the most serious and should be prevented and monitored. The main defect that hinders healthcare is information quality. Many work hours are consumed and many patient delays arise from the need to find, check, and/or verify information. This constant hunting, checking, and clarifying may require full-time workers. While an individual clarification may appear minor, the waste from accumulated efforts is monumental.

Transportation

Transportation is the conveyance of materials, equipment, information, and patients through an organization. From a patient perspective, the movement of items or information rarely creates value; thus, transportation is considered a waste. Transportation consumes staff resources and time but does not directly meet customer needs. Motion is different from transportation. Motion involves the movement of staff; transportation is the movement of "stuff."

Consider a patient who appears for a surgical pre-admission visit. This patient must first present and be registered. He or she then goes to the laboratory for a blood test, then walks to diagnostic imaging for a chest x-ray. Finally, the patient

---

* Shingo, S. 1986. *Zero Quality Control, Source Inspection, and Poka-Yoke*. Productivity Press, Cambridge, MA, p. 45.

returns to the clinic for a nursing screen and pre- and post-surgical education, followed by a trip to a different office for a meeting with an anesthesiologist. Even with optimal utilization of the staff and a leveraged footprint of the facility, the patient requires a lot of transportation.

Great organizations work relentlessly to identify and eliminate waste. Operational waste presents itself in the seven common forms discussed above: overproduction, waiting, overprocessing, inventory, motion, defects, and transportation. Now that we have working definitions of the common forms of waste, we will discuss some tools to identify and then eliminate this waste.

Principles of Improvement: Lean DNA

After you practice identifying waste over time and feel comfortable with the VA and NVA concepts, waste will start to become obvious (remember the helpful fact that 95% of activities are NVAs). The harder task is eliminating the waste. Before we discuss that, we must understand five improvement principles ("Lean DNA") to help guide our thinking (Figure 2.5). Whenever we want to eliminate waste, we should use these principles of Lean DNA as a foundation. The five principles are flow, pull, defect-free, visual management, and kaizen. Let's review them in more detail.

Flow Concept

The starting point for making improvement is creating flow. People often think of flow as a means of lining up sequential activities in a continuous manner. In healthcare, we want to flow patients though our system. Lining up all the activities to occur one after another would be a great improvement albeit very difficult to accomplish. However, the concept of flow is more than continuous processing of tasks. The Lean definition of flow is completing the VA tasks in continuous flow at the rate of customer demand in a standardized way.

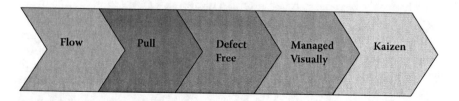

Figure 2.5 Lean DNA principles.

Linking the VA steps together implies that we have eliminated the NVA activities between the steps. It would not make sense to link all the tasks together in continuous flow. Why would we want to expend resources completing NVA work?

Assume that we have eliminated some waste and have linked the value-added tasks together. For an x-ray, assume that the technologist can perform the examination and immediately have a radiologist read the films and have results available for review by the ordering physician. This would be the usual flow in practice. Now we must ensure that this new process is capable of meeting customer demand. If this process can be repeated 32 times in an 8-hour shift and the patient demand is 40 per shift, we still have not satisfied the principle of flow. A process meeting the spirit of flow must be paced to the rate of customer demand.

Finally, assume we have now lined up the VA steps and devised a process capable of meeting customer demand. However, due to variation in the process, the outcomes vary. If we do not perform the activities in a standard way and achieve consistent outcomes, we have not met the spirit of flow. A process flows when the VA activities are lined up one after another, with no waiting or inventory between steps. The process will be capable of meeting customer demand and the work will be done in a standardized way to produce consistent outcomes.

Pull System

It may not be possible to create continuous flow of all steps. Constrained resources that are rarely used can make continuous flow very difficult. An example would be a patient arriving in the ER after being hit in the mouth with a baseball. The patient is in need of a dental surgeon adept at plastic procedures. How many ERs have one of these on staff? The work will stop until the referral is made and the specialist responds. The principle of pull enables the linkage of areas of continuous flow.

The concept of pull comes from the supermarket industry. How does the grocer know when to stock a shelf? The answer is when there is an empty space. How did the empty space get there? Consumers put items in their grocery carts for purchase. The signal to restock is removal of an item from a shelf.

This simple concept is the basis for pull. Without a signal to replenish, what could happen? We could run out of product, causing a loss of sales or overstock the area, leading to spoilage or obsolescence (e.g., meats, dairy products, and produce). Overstocking causes us to lose time, space, and resources while failing to meet the customers' need. This is the waste of overproduction, and pull was designed to prevent overproduction. Conversely, understocking creates wasted motion and unnecessary waiting.

Pull in its simplest form is a signal to do work. In the grocery store example, consumption is a signal to replenish. In Lean terms, the principle of pull implies that we would perform work only when we have a true need from the customer. To satisfy the principle of pull, the signal design should have certain attributes. The first is standardizing the signal to one type. Despite multiple ways to trigger any form of work, pull requires a single trigger.

As an example, consider healthcare referral workflow. On an inpatient medical floor, assume we must trigger an occupational therapist (OT) to perform an assessment. We could page the OT, call the OT, write a written referral, send an e-mail, make a face-to-face request, or trigger the referral during medical rounds. A great Lean organization has a *single* authoritative way to trigger referrals. Pick the best one for your organization. After you standardize the trigger, devise a single way to respond. How do you acknowledge a referral? We could again page, call, write, or otherwise convey the acknowledgment, but a great pull system has one way to trigger and one way to respond.

A good pull system also has positive attributes such as seamless and synchronized processes and involves no gaps, overproduction, asking, searching, or clarifying. An example of a good healthcare pull signal is placing physician orders in an "orders to be entered" basket for entry into the system. The only way to trigger the work is placing an order in the basket. The only response is pulling an order from the basket. Assuming the order entry system has other resources, response time can be standardized to achieve nearly (but not fully) continuous flow.

Other examples of using pull signals in healthcare include:

- Triggering a consult for a specialty not in house
- Triggering a service referral for home care
- Using a visual queue to know when to porter the next patient for a procedure
- Triggering a room clean following a discharge
- Triggering the build of OR case carts for the next 2 hours
- Using the supermarket concept to trigger replenishment of medicines, supplies, and equipment
- Triggering a physician to see the next patient in a clinic
- Making results available to trigger reassessment

There are literally thousands of examples, and a great Lean organization utilizes the principle of pull to link steps together whenever work cannot flow continuously.

Defect-Free Work

Assume that we have begun to design our work process and implemented pockets of continuous flow; where we could not create continuous flow, we established pull systems to link our areas of continuous flow together. So far so good. Will it matter that the work flows continuously and is tightly linked with pull systems if the outcomes are wrong? Definitely not. Negative outcomes in healthcare can be very serious. In fact our first mission in healthcare is to do no harm!

To prevent negative outcomes, we utilize the defect-free principle. In Lean terms, defect-free operation means doing work in a way that meets customer-specified quality requirements the first time. As the work moves from step to step, quality is designed into the process so the outcomes are consistent, meet customer requirements, and can be completed without rework and inspection. Some of the attributes of defect-free work are absence of errors, no need for rework, standardized procedures, quality at the source, non-personality based action, and absence of overprocessing and redundancy.

Expanding on the defect-free principle, there are several design approaches to allowing value to be delivered defect free. A few examples are detailed in Figure 2.6. Countless other tools may be used to deliver zero defects. Many of these are also used for total quality management approaches and for meeting certification and accreditation standards.

Visual Management

After a process has been designed using the principles of flow, pull, and defect-free, we need a system to manage the process. A Lean system is designed to be managed visually. Visual management allows everyone to distinguish normal from abnormal conditions. What kinds of activities are we interested in managing visually? Almost anything. Are we ahead of or behind the schedule? Is everyone following the standard work? Are all materials, supplies, and equipment in correct locations. Do we have suitable spaces for everything? What are the top three problems we are working on? Who is responsible for corrective actions? When will they be completed? What have the results been for the last month? Are we on budget? All these issues can be managed visually.

A visual management system should have certain attributes. The first is total transparency. This means that everyone has the ability to distinguish normal from abnormal in 5 seconds or less. No one should have to run a report or open a drawer to determine whether a status is normal or abnormal. Figure 2.7 illustrates a very simple example of transparency.

In this example, the person responsible for stocking supplies in a treatment room overfilled the cupboard with blue pads. In fact, this person normally filled the entire bottom shelf with blue pads. Adding a fill line to the cupboard allows the stocking person to determine at a glance whether the pads must be restocked and how many are needed. How much obsolescence of inventory have you noted in your organization?

Concept	Description
Successive Staff Checks	Each staff member checks the previous work before adding their own value. This insures that work is not completed in addition to previous work that may have a defect.
5S	Create a high performing work area that designs the work space, tools, supplies, equipment and information in a way that enables the work to be done defect free (more in Chapter 3).
Operational Methods Sheets	A visual tool that explains the work to be done at the task level, defines the quality specifications of the work, and shows the checks the staff member must take to insure the work is defect free. This approach ties closely with Successive Staff Checks.
Andon	Andon loosely translates to stopping the line. This is a management principle where the staff stops performing work when a defect is found and will not begin performing work again until a countermeasure is in place to prevent further defects. This creates time to identify the root cause of the problem, allowing for a permanent solution to be found.
Poka-Yoke	Poka-Yoke loosely translates to mistake proofing. This concept is in action when work is designed to make it impossible to do the work improperly. A simple example would be designing a date field so that the field has to be filled out in a computer screen before going to the next field. This mistake proofs leaving the field empty, preventing an error from occurring.
7 Quality Tools	The seven tools include the cause and effect diagram, the check sheet, the control chart, the histogram, the Pareto diagram, the scatter diagram, and the flowchart. These tools are used to explain what is happening in a system and are used because they do not require a lot of statistical training for the user. They are used frequently in healthcare to explain and interpret data.
Cause and Effect Diagram	Expanding on one of the seven quality tools, the cause and effect diagram, or Ishikawa diagram or fishbone diagram, is used to determine causes of problems and helps sort the problems into useful categories.

Figure 2.6   Defect-free concepts.

Concept	Description
5 Whys	This is a technique used to determine the root cause of a problem. By asking Why five different times it is possible to get to the underlying source of the problem so a solution can be identified that permanently solves the problem. Here is one of my favorite examples to this approach in practice.
	Scenario: The Washington Monument in Washington DC had to be refaced because of damage.
	Why 1: Why did the monument get damaged?
	Answer 1: Because the pigeons were leaving droppings on the surface.
	Why 2: Why were the pigeons leaving droppings on the surface?
	Answer 2: Because they were in the area.
	Why 3: Why were the pigeons in the area?
	Answer 3: Because they were eating bugs?
	Why 4: Why were bugs there?
	Answer 4: Because they were attracted to the light.
	Why 5: Why were the bugs attracted to the monument lights?
	Answer 5: Because the monument lights were the first lights on in the area.
	Solution: Turn the monument spotlights on 30 minutes later.
	I'll bet this wasn't the answer you expected. When you get the direct cause, the answer is usually quite a bit different than taking the first solution that jumps in our heads.
FMEA	Failure Mode Effects Analysis is a tool used to mitigate risk. The process involves reviewing each step and determining the potential sources of failure. Each failure is assigned a risk priority number (RPN) that is the product of the severity (SEV) of the failure, the frequency (FREQ) of the failure, and the ability to detect (DET) the failure on scale of 0 to 10. (RPN = SEV x FREQ x DET) The goal of using the FMEA is to design solutions to mitigate the risk before implementation. This approach is highly recommended on any activity that has impacts on patient safety. A target for improvement using an FMEA approach would be to reduce the total RPN by 50%.

Figure 2.6 *(Continued)* **Defect-free concepts.**

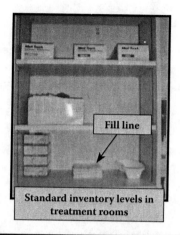

Figure 2.7 Setting inventory levels. (From HHCC kaizen, Setting inventory levels, *Headwaters*, 2009. With permission.)

Another attribute of visual management is that it triggers action. The system allows visualization of normal and abnormal. Another aspect is doing something about the abnormal. If we are behind, what is the intervention for catching up? If an item is not in its correct place, who will find it and return it to its home? Many Lean visual management systems operate exactly as designed, but the staff and management fail to take action. We'll explore some visual management systems later when we review the common tools for seeing and eliminating waste and discuss case studies.

In working with healthcare organizations, I spend nearly 50% of my time teaching line management, middle management, and senior management how to understand and operate visual management systems. This topic is that important. A great design, effective flow and pull systems, and elimination of many defects do not matter if a system cannot be managed visually. The culture of your organization will always revert back to the previous status quo without a robust visual management system. Sound visual management is the key to sustainability.

Great organizations can distinguish normal from abnormal conditions at a glance, and take immediate action when abnormal conditions arise.

Kaizen

The fifth principle of improvement is kaizen. As noted earlier, it is a combination of "kai" meaning *change* and "zen" meaning *for the better*. To create a culture of improvement, we must build a system that improves continuously. Great organizations get better every day and their employees and managers leave their workplaces in better shape than when they arrived. Imagine what that could look like!

The practice of kaizen involves making small, incremental, continuous changes to our work to deliver more value to the customer. The results include eliminating NVA activities, creating better standard work, relocating items to minimize wasted movement, and mistake proofing a process to eliminate defects.

In the spirit of practicing kaizen, Lean organizations frequently benchmark, but not in the areas you might think. Actually two types of benchmarking occur. The first is benchmarking against perfection: delivering all VA activities via continuous flow with no defects. When you compare your current performance against perfection, you will see that you have much to improve. This comparison of current performance against perfection can create a state of tension that spurs further improvement.

The second benchmark is against the best in the world. Great organizations compare their processes against industries with world class performance. How does your performance in infection prevention compare with safe drinking water? How does your quality in medicine administration compare with the safe practices of a nuclear power plant? You can compare your organization to other healthcare organizations, but I am not aware of any citation of healthcare performance benchmarks as the best in the world. Do not compare your organization with similar operations; look beyond healthcare. Healthcare should aspire to the standards of certain industry examples. This is not meant to put healthcare beneath other industries; it is intended to give you a different vision for what is possible. Practice kaizen. Improve every day.

You never get to a state of Lean. If it is not broke, fix it anyway. If it runs well, improve it. *Never* be satisfied with current performance. Challenge the management, staff, and medical practitioners to do better. When you create a mindset of continuous improvement, you are meeting the spirit of kaizen.

Chapter 3

Tools for Improvement

Introduction to Tools

Excellence comes from repeatedly eliminating non-value-added (NVA) activities in every process across an organization. To see and eliminate these activities, we need tools to assist us. While we have literally hundreds to choose from, certain tools lend themselves to frequent application in Lean improvement. I refer to them as the common tools to see and eliminate waste and they include:

- Takt time
- Direct (time) observation
- Loading diagram
- Spaghetti mapping and circle diagrams
- Flow diagram with value-added and non-value-added analysis
- Standard work
- Process control

All these tools are intuitive in design and relatively easy to use. You do not need special mathematics skills, a computer, or an advanced education to use them. In a great Lean organization, all of the staff and management effectively use these tools and they can be applied *anywhere* work is done.

It is fundamental that managers and leaders understand and can teach the common tools because their ability to do so is a key factor in their success. In a Lean environment, we expect leaders to be coaches and mentors. Development of staff is accelerated when a manager can ask the right question that can guide the thinking of a staff member or team. In a Lean environment, that ability to ask the right question comes from a deep understanding of the principles and tools. This understanding is best developed in a "learn by doing" environment, where the tools can be practiced, mastered, and eventually taught.

Before I explain the tools and their use in healthcare, I suggest you keep a few points in mind. First, while the tools are easy to use, their applications vary widely. It takes a decade or more to understand all the applications of the tools. This learning curve is likely even steeper in healthcare, considering the industry's complexity, ever-changing technology, and increasing specialization of care. Second, it can be challenging to determine which tool to use and when to use it. Novice Lean practitioners frequently select the wrong tool or apply a tool improperly, leading to minimized results and a frustrated team. An old saying is, "When all you have is a hammer, everything looks like a nail." Make sure you have a full set of tools, not just a hammer.

Let's explore the individual tools and some of their applications.

Takt Time

"Takt" is derived from the German *taktzeit*, which is loosely translated as "rhythm" or "beat." Takt time is a mathematical formula that reveals the rhythm of output of goods and services. Just as the heartbeat regulates the flow of blood through the body, Takt time acts as the heartbeat of a process and the formula is:

Takt time = Time available to do work ÷ volume of work to be completed

Calculating this formula is the first step in improving your process. Many decisions and design attributes will be predicated on this time. Staffing calculations, process monitoring, supply chain management, and space planning all derive from this calculation. Let's execute some takt time calculations in both clinical and administrative settings.

Clinic Example

A dermatology clinic operates from 9 a.m. until 5 p.m., Monday through Friday, but the clinic is not available to see patients for a half hour between 12:00 noon and 12:30 p.m. Daily customer demand is based on 18 new patients who need to see the doctor and 14 patients for follow-up visits. Takt time calculations for this scenario are:

Available time = 8 hours (9 a.m. to 5 p.m.) − 0.5 hour for lunch
= 7.5 hours or 450 minutes daily

Volume of work = 18 new patients + 14 follow-up patients = 32 patients

Takt time (Tt) = 450 minutes ÷ 32 patients
= 14.0625 minutes, rounded to 14 minutes

What does 14 minutes mean? Many people believe this result assumes that every patient must be seen, assessed, treated, and discharged in 14 minutes—14 minutes is the entire visit time. This assumption is incorrect.

Takt time describes the rhythm of the process: a new patient must enter (register in) the system every 14 minutes and a discharged patient must depart the clinic every 14 minutes. The time spent by the patient in the clinic is not relevant to the takt time. This total time spent in the clinic has implications for staffing, space requirements, and resources consumed, but not for takt time.

What happens if the operation runs ahead of or behind the calculated takt time? What if a patient enters and leaves the clinic, say, every 15 minutes (behind schedule) or every 13 minutes (ahead of schedule)? It is very important to understand the implications of these very real possibilities.

If a new patient does not enter and exit the clinic every 14 minutes, the work will simply not be done on time. As a result, patients experience longer wait times as the healthcare team struggles to catch up. (If you ever go to a clinic for a 1:00 p.m. appointment, only to be seen by a physician at 2:30 p.m., you are experiencing what happens when a clinic runs behind takt time.) In this case, the work is not complete at 5 p.m. and staff must be paid overtime to get it done.

Assuming we are running a process in a standardized way, we cannot simply work faster and catch up. Each task requires a certain amount of time and skipping parts of the task result in quality errors and mistakes. Rushing is also noticed by patients. I frequently hear patients complain they did not have enough time during a visit to have all their questions answered.

It is possible to add resources and catch up, but how many operations have extra staff, providers, and rooms you can activate when they are behind schedule?

We understand the results of exceeding takt time. What happens when we run ahead of takt time? Intuitively, you might think this is a good result: every task would occur on time and no patients would be waiting! However, from a Lean thinking perspective, running ahead of takt time is not a smart way to run a business. Running ahead of takt time indicates that we have idle resources, and/or we are skipping important steps. How do we know that? This concept will become clearer as we examine two more essential Lean tools: direct observation and the loading diagram.

Lean organizations strive to run exactly to takt time all the time. In practice, novice organizations find running to takt time extremely difficult. Waste is the factor that most frequently prevents organizations from running to takt time. Waste consistently creeps into the process, causing even the most hardworking teams to miss their takt time targets. This is why we must diligently strive to make the waste visible so we can address problems in real time. Measuring performance against the takt time makes this possible. Let's look at a few more scenarios. Calculate the takt times based on the process information provided.

Scenario A: Administration (Coding) — Four full-time associates work on coding and 150 completed cases must be coded daily. Staff members work 8.5-hour shifts (less two 15-minute breaks and 30-minute unpaid lunches). What is the takt time for the coding process? Here is the calculation:

$$\text{Available time (At)} = 8.5 \text{ hours} - 1 \text{ hour}$$
$$(\text{two 15-minute breaks and 30-minute lunch})$$
$$= 7.5 \text{ hours or } 450 \text{ minutes}$$

$$\text{Volume or demand (V)} = 150 \text{ cases per day}$$

$$\text{Takt time (Tt)} = \text{Available time (450 minutes)} \div 150 \text{ cases} = 3 \text{ minutes}$$

Discussion point: Staffing levels are irrelevant in a takt time calculation.

Scenario B: Administration (Human Resources, Recruiting) — Over the next fiscal quarter (90 days), 18 staff members will retire. Additionally, four new budgeted positions will be posted and need to be filled. What is the takt time for the recruiting process to fill 22 positions? Here is the calculation:

$$\text{Available time (At)} = 90 \text{ days or } 12 \text{ weeks}$$

$$\text{Volume or demand (V)} = 22 \text{ positions}$$

$$\text{Takt time (Tt)} = 12 \text{ weeks} \div 22 \text{ positions}$$
$$= 0.55 \text{ week or about } 1/2 \text{ week per position}$$

Discussion point: Use relevant units when considering time. Calculating time in minutes or seconds would not have been helpful in this scenario.

Scenario C: Clinical (Diagnostic Imaging, CT Scanning) — The CT scanning department has two scanners. Both machines run for 9-hour shifts. The staff staggers breaks and lunches and the machines are never stopped during the two shifts. Collectively, the two machines have capacity to complete 48 examinations per day (45-minute exams are scheduled across both machines). The patient referrals come in at a rate of 58 exams per day so there is a wait list for examinations. Assume for this example that the number of exams equals the number of referrals. What is the takt time for CT scanning? Here is the calculation:

Available time (At) = 18 hours or 1080 minutes (2 shifts × 9 hours)

Volume or demand (V) = 58 referrals

Takt time (Tt) = 1080 minutes ÷ 58 referrals = 18.6 minutes per examination

Discussion point: Volume is based on demand. Did you use the scanner capacity of 48 exams per day instead of the demand of 58 referrals in the calculation? The number of resources (equipment and people) is not relevant for takt time calculation.

You can see that the applications for takt time are quite diverse. Takt time can be calculated in any unit of time although the smallest unit of meaningful time is the preferred method (if you can calculate in minutes or hours, use minutes). Virtually all mathematical calculations of waste begin with the determination of takt time. I recommend you begin any Lean work with a takt time calculation. Look at the problem your department or clinic faces, determine the issues that require takt time calculation, and proceed from there. Determining whether the operation runs ahead of or behind takt time uncovers your first opportunity for improvement. Great organizations run exactly to takt time and use the exact number of resources needed to meet the demand. The next two tools (direct observations and loading diagrams) show us how to match the takt time with the correct quantity of resources.

Direct (Time) Observation

The best way to see waste is "up close and personal" by directly observing processes. To review, wastes occur through waiting, motion, transportation, overprocessing, overproduction, defects, and inventory. We want to find examples of all of these forms of waste, up close, in a healthcare environment.

Many teams bring reams of data to improvement activities, for example, averages, standard deviations, minimums, maximums, medians, and modes. We can learn a lot from such data but data does not reveal waste. To identify waste, we must go where work is done and see the waste directly. In Lean terminology, the place where work is done is the *gemba*. Typically, after you observe 10 cycles of a process, you will have observed more than enough waste.

During normal workdays, many managers go into their work areas, usually to find the answer to a question, speak to someone, or assign a task. These are all important work-related duties required during a work week. What many managers fail to do during visits to their work areas is see waste. As a practical exercise, separate yourself from your to-do list and go observe the work in progress.

Time Observation

Process:							Observer						Date:	
Step #	Work Element	1	2	3	4	5	6	7	8	9	10	11	12	Task Time	Remarks

Lowest repeatable Cycle time

Time for 1 Cycle

Figure 3.1   Blank time observation form.

What do you really see? Remember, you are looking for waste in the forms of motion, transportation, overprocessing, overproduction, waiting, defects, and inventory. No matter what work you do in any aspect of the healthcare system (or other business endeavor), I guarantee that you will find waste, but you must train yourself to find it.

If you go to the gemba (the place where work is done) with the intent to see waste, you will suddenly see more than you ever thought was present. Sure, you will see lots of busy staff and several patients and their family members, but will you see someone actually adding value? Lean improvement starts with direct observation and then goes one step further. Waste shows up as lost time. Units of time are added to direct observations to quantify waste. Lean practitioners use observation forms to document wastes observed and the corresponding times involved. Figure 3.1 is a blank observation form.

Before we get too far into the details of time observation, we should discuss what the time observation is and is not. As an industrial engineering major, I have a deep appreciation for time studies and time-and-motion studies. Time studies are often used to break work down into increments as small as 1/100 of a second. Adjustments to standards are sometimes based on fatigue as a worker tires throughout a work day. Scientific measurement is a valuable tool for improving productivity and was developed at the turn of the twentieth century by Frederick Taylor, the father of scientific management. Scientific management was improved through the application of motion studies. Frank and Lillian Gilbreth are considered the pioneers of motion study. They watched the way bricklayers worked and characterized 18 basic hand motions. Studying hand motion allowed them to reduce motion, simultaneously improving productivity and decreasing fatigue.[*]

The practice of scientific measurement via time and motion studies eventually evolved into a process known as a time study. The first step of a time study (different from direct observation) is recording task times. Next, the work is standardized, usually in a more productive and safer way. Finally a time standard is established for the "average" worker performing a task at a reasonable rate. Individual performance is then measured against this standard and is frequently expressed as a percentage. For example, Bill performs at 120% of standard. This implies that Bill's productivity is 20% higher than the corporate standard. Employee compensation systems were built around their performances against standards. When combined with a piece rate incentive, working better than standard appeared to be lucrative.

Here's the problem. Have you ever met an average worker? What does one look like? When I managed operations, I didn't want an average team. I wanted a team of superstars and so do you. The truth is most workers are already superstars. Later in this chapter we will talk about standard work and how all workers can be superstars every day. In a Lean environment, we expect everyone to work to the cycle time required to meet takt time every time they complete a task. To do this we must eliminate waste, not work harder. Direct observation helps us see waste and quantify it in time units.

If you're concerned that you may need an engineering degree before successfully going Lean, don't despair! Fortunately, direct observation is a lot simpler than a time-and-motion study. We don't have to be trained industrial engineers; we simply need to be healthcare professionals seeking to get better. With that in mind, let's review a completed time observation so we can learn how to use the tool. This observation involves the work of an RN during a clinic visit. Before completing a time observation form (Figure 3.2), we want to first observe a few cycles so we can see the repeating pattern of work. Then we want to document the task steps on the form. Now we can begin to observe the process and capture the time elements.

---

[*] Salvendy, G., Ed. 1982. *Handbook of Industrial Engineering.* John Wiley & Sons, New York, pp. 4.5.1–4.5.2.

Time Observation

Process:	RN CLINIC VISIT						Observer	P. SMITH				Date: 7 FEB 2011	
Step #	Work Element	1	2	3	4	5	6	7	8	9	10	11	12	Task Time	Remarks
1	Meet patient, walk to room	24 / (24)	27 / 27	25 / 25	27 / 27	24 / (24)								:24	Can Clerk escort patient ?
2	Initial assessment & charting	2:24 / (2:00)	2:15 / 1:48	2:20 / 1:55	2:27 / (2:00)	2:14 / 1:50								2:00	chart while Assessing
3	Gather supplies for procedure	4:14 / (1:50)	4:10 / 1:55	4:20 / 2:00	4:12 / (1:50)	4:24 / 2:10								1:50	move supplies to room
4	Treatment & chart	10:16 / 6:02	11:15 / 7:05	10:30 / (6:10)	10:41 / 6:28	10:38 / (6:10)								6:10	
5	deliver D/C instructions & chart	12:27 / 2:09	13:05 / 1:50	12:31 / (2:05)	12:30 / (2:05)	12:44 / 2:10								2:05	
6	Escort patient to front desk	12:58 / :31	13:28 / (2:27)	12:55 / :20	13:15 / (2:27)	13:14 / :30								:25	Can Patient leave on their own ?
	Time for 1 Cycle	12:58	13:38	12:55	13:15	13:14								12:54 ←	Lowest repeatable Cycle time

Figure 3.2 Completed time observation form.

After you acquire the 10 (or more) observations, you can start analyzing the data. Across each row, look for numbers that repeat. The two lowest numbers that repeat indicate the time to be applied to the task and are written into the "Task Time" column. Totaling the task numbers gives us a standard for current operations. In our example, the standard process time is 12:54 for the RN work associated with a clinic visit. Keep in mind that we have not yet removed waste from the process. Time observation results are often smaller than you would think. Many teams are amazed at the time results because they anticipate wider variations in task times. The following suggestions for direct observation may be helpful:

1. Generally, 10 observations are sufficient to capture (identify) waste. For some processes like triage and patient registration, observations can be achieved in a short time. However, 10 observations of more complex processes such as following a care pathway for community-acquired pneumonia may take a week or longer.
2. I prefer two-person teams for performing time observation. One person runs the watch and the other holds the clipboard.

3. Do not be concerned about variations. All processes are repeatable. Enough observations will allow you to see a pattern.

4. A video camera is useful for observing long cycle times with lots of waiting. You can fast-forward through the slow-moving activities (usually waiting between steps). This technique is also helpful for analyzing turnaround times for preparing operating rooms and cleaning patient rooms. You can replay the video as needed to capture in detail the wasted time and steps traveled.

5. Always put the people you are observing at ease before you perform a time observation. Most people are not comfortable when a team shows up with stopwatches and clipboards! Take a few moments to explain what you are doing and why. Many people have seen time studies that were followed by reductions in staff and may feel anxious as a result. A simple explanation will help. Remember, you are looking for waste. Also, be sure to obtain patient and/or family consent before timing a patient.

6. Understand the timing subject. Are you timing the staff, the patient, or the process? You may want to observe the cycle time of a staff worker. This is the total time required for an associate to complete one cycle of a process. If more than one person is involved, each person requires a separate time observation. For example, in a clinic visit, we would complete time observations of registration, nursing, and physician processes.

You may want to analyze the lead time of a process. Lead is the total time between "customer need" and "customer need met." As an example, what is the total lead time for a patient during a clinic visit? Although registration took only 4 minutes, the nursing cycle time was 12 minutes, and the physician cycle time was 10 minutes (total of 26 minutes), the total lead time for the patient was 90 minutes. Where did that time come from? To capture lead time, we must perform a time observation of the patient. What is the patient doing most of the time he or she is in the clinic? Waiting. To summarize, the best way to see waste is to directly observe processes. We go to the gemba for a firsthand view of wastes during daily operations. To quantify the waste, we assign times to activities using time observation forms.

Loading Diagram

A loading diagram tool may also be called a cycle time/takt time bar chart. One question that frequently arises during studies aimed at improvement is the size of the staff needed to run an operation. A variety of work measurement tools exist to help answer this question and several are electronic. Lean organizations use the data from the takt time calculation and the time observation recordings to solve this problem.

We begin with a simple example. We are now the proud owners of a sandwich shop. During lunch, we must service one customer per minute because 60 people walked through our door during a lunch hour. Based on these conditions, our takt time is 1 minute; the available time is 60 minutes; and the demand is 60 sandwiches. Assume that it takes 2 minutes to service a customer (45 seconds to cut and toast the bread. 45 seconds to add the meat and vegetables, and 30 seconds to collect the cash and return the change.

How many people are needed to service a customer every minute? If a single person handles every customer from start to finish, the operation will quickly fall behind. Moving a single customer through the process every 2 minutes will not work if new customers appear at 1-minute intervals and we will need more space for people to wait. If two people work together (one employee, one customer; second employee, second customer), we meet the available time of 2 minutes per customer. On average, we will flow one customer though the process every minute and remain on time. A better answer is to create continuous flow—a system used in Subway sandwich shops. One employee processes the first minute's worth of work and the next employee handles the second minute's worth of work. This system will flow one customer per minute through the process.

The important issue is the correlation between the cycle time (2 minutes of processing per customer) and the takt time (1 minute between customers). If we take the sum of the cycle times for a process and divide it by the takt time, we can determine minimum staffing. In this case, minimum staffing = Σcycle times $\div$ takt time = 2 minutes $\div$ 1 minute = 2 staff. Remember that takt time is crucial to Lean improvement. Understanding takt time is critical for appropriately staffing a work area.

The tool that shows the relationship between cycle time (Ct) and takt time (Tt) is a loading diagram, also known as a cycle time/takt time bar chart. Figure 3.3 shows an example. To complete a loading diagram, first calculate the takt time. Then using a dashed red line, draw the takt time on the y-axis formatted to time increments After adding the takt time line, show the cycle times by person along the x-axis. Each person gets a bar. The final step is calculating minimum staffing by adding the cycle times of each person and dividing the total by the takt time. In Figure 3.3, the sum of the cycle times is 14.62 minutes and the takt time is 3.5 minutes. Thus the minimum staffing is 14.62 $\div$ 3.5 = 4.18 (rounded to 4.2) staff.

Now that we have completed a loading diagram, we can perform some analysis. How is each person's cycle time loaded against the takt time? Are the individual cycle times greater than the takt time? If so, the process is running behind. Are any individual cycle times below the takt time? If so, they may represent underutilized resources. How does actual staffing compare to the calculated minimum staffing? Are you overstaffed?

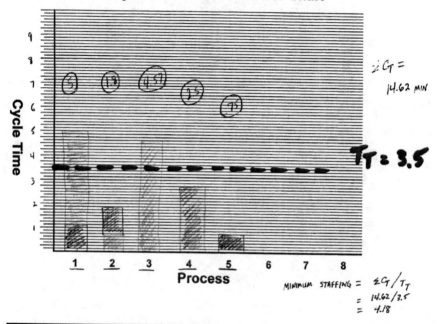

Figure 3.3 **Loading diagram.**

We can learn plenty from a loading diagram. This tool highlights waste in different areas, mostly related to staffing. Figure 3.3 indicates that 4.2 staffing is required but the process actually operates with a staff of 5.

The first step in using a loading diagram to make improvement is eliminating waste. The result of eliminating waste should be corresponding reductions in cycle times that will appear on a loading diagram as smaller bars (lower individual cycle times).

After we eliminate the waste, we want to create standard operations to prevent future waste. (Standard work will be discussed later in this chapter.) Finally, we want to balance the work: moving segments of the remaining work to create an even distribution of time. Ideally, all employees should be equally loaded against takt time. Figure 3.4 shows the actions taken to create standard operations. After completing these three activities, you will then create a new loading diagram and a new staffing plan. The results will be similar to those in Figure 3.5.

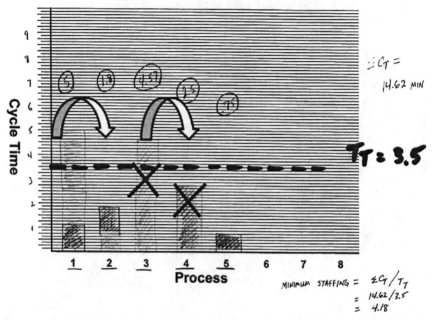

Figure 3.4   Eliminating waste and line balancing.

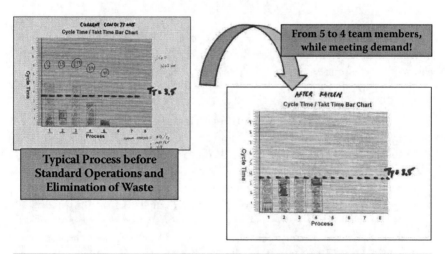

Figure 3.5   Loading diagram after waste elimination, standard operation, and line balancing.

The figure indicates that two meaningful improvements were realized. With the reduction of NVA activities, the total cycle dropped to 14 minutes and allowed a reduction of minimum staff from 5 to 4—a 20% reduction. By balancing the work, patient throughput was reduced from one patient every 5 minutes to one patient every 3.5 minutes—a 30% improvement.

Understanding a loading diagram is key to both flow and productivity. The following suggestions will help you to prepare and use a loading diagram:

1. When completing the cycle time bars, use different colors for the different steps. This helps to reveal the impact of eliminating waste and helps balance the work.
2. A loading diagram is a key to productivity. Great organizations understand the tool and staff to the data it reveals.
3. Some operations are not candidates for balancing. In healthcare, the scope of practice is a legitimate barrier to line balancing. Only a physician can do a physician's job. Hospitals must allow for a wide range of professional positions that require high levels of specialization. Despite these limitations, management can always find opportunities to move work around or reallocate areas of responsibility—particularly for administrative work, handling supplies, and cleaning equipment.
4. If a loading diagram shows that a professional is not loaded against takt time, assigning that person a non-professional task is acceptable. I frequently hear that, "We don't want nurses portering patients." This issue is controversial, but in the opinions of expert Lean practitioners, it is better to have nurses porter patients if they have time and the task will not affect other areas of their work, than add a hand-off and introduce another non-professional resource to the system.
5. Staffing calculations rarely yield whole numbers and usually require "rounding up" or "rounding down." Consider minimum staffing = $\Sigma Ct/Tt$ = 46.5 minutes/8.3 minutes = 5.60 people. How do we staff 0.60 of a person? Table 3.1 may serve as a guideline for staffing considerations.
6. Assuming that people want to pursue training and take vacations, you will need to carry more staff than the minimum staffing calculation indicates. I recommend that your full time staff be the minimum staffing calculation divided by 0.85. This will give you a good starting point. Depending on the seniority of your workforce and access to part time staffing, you may adjust this number up or down.

Spaghetti Mapping and Circle Diagrams

Two waste areas that can be quickly observed are motion and transportation. Remember that motion is staff movement in excess of what is needed to deliver

Table 3.1 Calculating Minimum Staffing

Minimum Staffing Calculation	Rounding	Key Points
End with 0.25 of a person or less (example: minimum staffing = 4.18 people)	Round total staffing down to 4	Try to eliminate more waste to achieve capable process at lower number
More than 0.25 to 0.67 of a person (example: minimum staffing = 4.58 people)	Run process with a partial person who has available time but is not fully loaded	Flex a person in and out of the process based on demand
More than 0.67 of a person (example: minimum staffing = 4.83 people)	Round total staffing up to 5	For continuous improvement, try to remove more waste during next study

value; transportation is the movement of "stuff." Both activities consume time, space and resources, but do not directly contribute to meeting customer needs. Spaghetti mapping is so named because the end product of the activity looks like a plate of spaghetti.

Figure 3.6 is an example of a spaghetti map showing the travel motion of an associate working in a receiving department. In slightly more than 10 minutes of observation, the associate walked over 561 feet. We can learn a great deal from this tool. Why did the receiving associate have to leave his area? Why are the distances so far? Is this part of a normal receiving cycle or did something happen to create the need for the associate to walk? How much time was lost as a result of the walking? A spaghetti map makes waste visible so that it can be eliminated. A spaghetti map can also be used to show transportation waste. Follow the path of an IV solution or suture through your organization. How far does it travel? How many times is it picked up and put down before it is used on a patient?

Start at the receiving dock and trace the path of an item. The number of steps travelled and the number of times the product is handled may surprise you. A spaghetti map makes all this waste visible. To complete a spaghetti map, you need sophisticated tools: a pencil and paper. Draw a general footprint of the facility or area to be covered. Having a scaled map of the area is not essential, but determining distances traveled is easier if you have access to blueprints. Follow the path of the staff associate if you are trying to capture the waste of motion. Follow the path of an item or patient if you want to find waste of transportation. These processes are not mutually exclusive. You can do both.

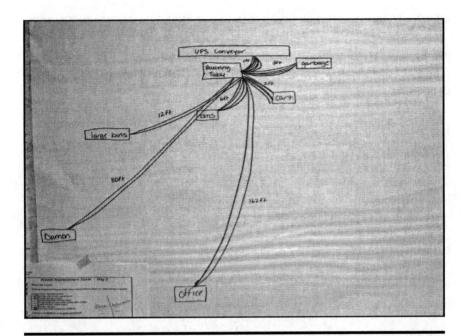

Figure 3.6 Spaghetti map. (Kaizen event report—spaghetti report. With permission.)

Each line on the map represents a move or conveyance and corresponding stop in the process. You can summarize the distance by walking the steps or converting the path to distance using the scale on a drawing or a measurement wheel. A reasonable goal for improvement is a 50% reduction in the number of moves and a 50% reduction in distance traveled for the process under study. A spaghetti map makes wastes of motion and transportation visible.

Circle Diagram

Sometimes movements are less visible. How do we capture the wasted motion and transportation of information? If the information is contained on paper, capturing motion and transportation is not difficult; we can follow the paper flow using a spaghetti map. But what about the electronic flow of information via faxes, e-mails, and computer programs? To capture the waste of transactions (a transaction is *transportation* of electronic information), we use a tool called a circle diagram (Figure 3.7).

Each time information is exchanged or an electronic transaction occurs, a line is drawn across a circle. Start a diagram by drawing a large circle on a piece of flip chart paper. At random locations around the outside, note the different

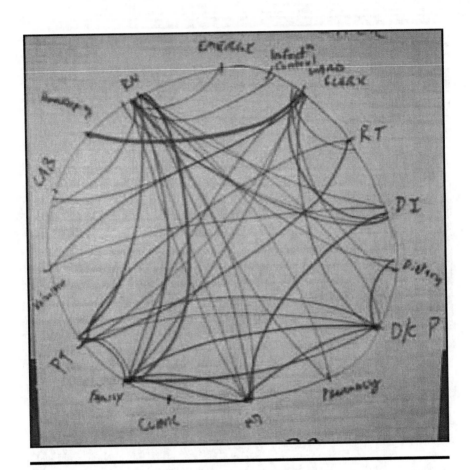

Figure 3.7　Circle diagram.

functions (people) exchanging information. To determine the number of hand-offs, count the lines on the paper. The figure example describes the flow of information involved in collaborative care planning for an internal medicine patient. In this case, the process involved more than 40 hand-offs.

Of course, many processes are very complex and require many hand-offs. But what do you think of the quality of information exchanged more than 40 times? Do you remember playing "broken telephone" in grade school? The goal was to communicate a sentence through many students and hopefully the sentence at the end would be the same as the sentence at the start. The first student is given a phrase by the teacher. The student then repeats the phrase (exactly as delivered and only once) to the next student. The process repeats until each child has a chance to repeat exactly what he or she heard from the previous child. By the end of the game, the phrase is completely different. It's a fun way to demonstrate what we all know intuitively: human communication (passing of information) is prone to errors.

In a Lean organization, we want communication to be direct and simple. Fewer hand-offs and transactions are always better. A good improvement goal would be a 50% reduction in hand-offs. A circle diagram makes the waste of hand-offs visible so we can reduce the number required, and thus improve the quality of information while shortening the timeline.

Flow Diagram with Value-Added/ Non-Value-Added Analyses

One of the most helpful ways to understand process is to analyze the workflow. This analysis exposes the tasks performed, starts and stops in a process, waiting, connections, and hand-offs. The tool that Lean organizations use to help understand process is the flow diagram (also known as a process map). The first step is using sticky notes to define the task steps, then posting them on a wall so that the process will be visible to the entire team. Figure 3.8 is an example of a process map. Begin by clearly defining where the process begins and where it ends. This prevents the "scope creep" that plagues many teams as they begin the improvement process. To keep the process well defined and manageable, clearly establish the start and end points and focus all discussion and improvement between those points.

The starting and ending delineation can be somewhat arbitrary, but should be as inclusive as possible. To devise a process map for the laboratory, we could choose to begin when a specimen arrives and end (complete the map) when the result is available for review. This makes perfect sense from the laboratory perspective.

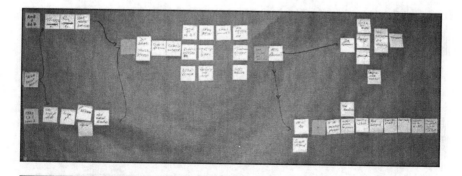

Figure 3.8　Process map.

What about the customer perspective? Let's look at the process from a more inclusive view. The customer process begins when the decision is made to order a test and ends when the results are reviewed. This process map would look entirely different from the first one. Since our role in improvement is to eliminate waste and deliver more value to the customer (patient), we always want to map through customer eyes.

It is also a good idea to have a flow diagram completed by the people who do the work. Management sometimes tries to steer mapping activity toward the should-be state instead of the as-is situation. Perceptions aside, we want to see how the process really operates to best uncover all the waste. The people who do the work can best define the as-is condition and do the mapping. Furthermore, the organization benefits from increased levels of employee buy-in. People always believe their own work.

Here's a final tip. Do not get obsessed with using proper flowchart symbols. If you have the skills to use them as you map, go ahead, but remember that the goal is to eliminate waste. We do not need symbols to see extra steps, missing steps, redundancy, waiting, checking, clarifying, and walking. Simple phrases on sticky notes can clearly show exactly where the waste is.

Value-Added and Non-Value-Added Analyses

After a process map has been completed, categorizing each step as a value-added or non-value-added activity helps the team understand how much non-value content exists. Colors on sticky notes may be used to denote the status of each task step, for example, green dots for value-added (VA) activities and red dots for non-value-added (NVA) activities. Dime-sized red and green dots on corners of sticky notes will not interfere with ability to read the notes. Figure 3.9 is an example of a flow diagram with the VA and NVA analysis completed.

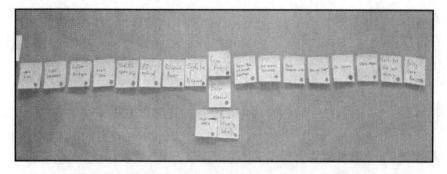

Figure 3.9   Value-added and non-value-added analysis.

Recall from Chapter 2 that most processes are 95% NVA and 5% VA. When analyzing VA versus NVA steps, expect nine parts NVA activities to one part VA activity. Our goal in Lean improvement is to see and eliminate NVA activities. The VA/NVA analysis makes the NVA activities visible. As a tip in completing this type of analysis, I recommend that you complete the flow diagram and the VA/NVA analysis activities in close sequence. After the flow diagram (process map) is completed, the VA/NVA analysis can begin. A second tip is to remember that VA and NVA contents are determined through customer eyes, not those of staffers.

Standard Work

After work has been analyzed and solutions tested, you need to create standard work. To explain that concept, we begin by defining a standard. Quite simply, a standard is a basis for comparison. An example of a standard is a length of 1 meter. The meter is a defined and well known standard for measuring distance. Another type is the time standard. We all understand what a minute is and share the same view of an hour. This is possible because we have a basis for comparison. Fundamentally, no improvement can occur unless standards exist. Without a standard, you have nothing against which to compare improvements; hence, no improvement.

Now that we have a working definition of a standard, we can discuss standard work from a Lean perspective. Masaki Imai's book titled *Gemba Kaizen* describes in great detail the needs for and benefits from workplace standards.[*] They:

1. Represent the best, easiest, and safest way to do a job
2. Offer the best way to preserve know-how and expertise
3. Provide a way to measure performance
4. Show the relationship between cause and effect
5. Provide a basis for both maintenance and improvement
6. Provide objectives and indicate training goals
7. Provide a basis for training
8. Create a basis for preventing recurrence of errors and minimizing variability

Standard work is like a recipe. If we follow the recipe, we create a consistent outcome. For example, if we bake pies by mixing the right ingredients in the right order in the right amounts and bake them at the correct temperature for the correct time, we produce pies that consistently look and taste great. Healthcare uses different recipes but the expectations are the same. If we follow the correct

---

[*] Imai, M. 1997. *Gemba Kaizen*, McGraw Hill, New York, pp. 54–56.

recipe for administering medication—correct order, material, and dosage delivered at the right time to the right patient—we achieve favorable outcomes. The first favorable outcome is patient safety; the second is production of the correct treatment effect.

Now consider delivering medicine differently. Assume we do not have a consistent recipe for administration. Different physicians and different nurses use different approaches to ensure that they follow the most current order. The safety systems in place to ensure that the right medicine is delivered to the right patient at the right time vary slightly. Some people recheck their steps; others take information at face value. Is it unrealistic to expect different outcomes? Perhaps a dose is missed or the dose is wrong because the order was updated but has not yet cycled through the system. The result may be an adverse drug event. Standard work ensures consistent and repeatable outcomes. This is another step in improvement.

In any work environment, the recipe represents the easiest, safest, and best known method of performing a task. In healthcare, many sources of evidence-based care are documented. The existence of many research organizations is based on developing standards for care. Some recipes, for example, administering CPR and performing proper hand hygiene, are well known. However, many facets of healthcare totally lack standards. What is the standard method for cleaning a patient room? What is the standard work for operating room turn-over? And most importantly: if there is a standard, is it consistently followed? We need only go back to the hand hygiene example to illustrate this point.

A Lean standard consists of three elements: takt time, work sequence, and standard work in process. You are already familiar with takt time, discussed in Chapter 2. Takt time is the lead calculation in Lean improvement and drives many of the other parts of a Lean system including standard work. Why is takt time part of standard work? When we use the common tools to see and eliminate waste, we complete a loading diagram to ensure that the staffing and cycle times for the work can be completed within the required takt time. The work standard that will be put into place must be capable of meeting the takt time. A work standard that is consistent but fails to meet customer demand is wasteful.

The work sequence is the next element of standard work. It is common to think of a set of tasks as standard work but in fact the work sequence (otherwise known as standard operating procedure) is not standard work, but only a piece of it. The work sequence is the set of tasks and corresponding times needed to complete them. Work should always be completed in the same order and in the same time increments to ensure a consistent and repeatable outcome. Sounds simple, right? You'll discover it's anything but.

Never underestimate your staff's emotional investment in their work sequences! Because of such emotional investment, achieving a single standard can be extremely difficult. Each staff member has his or her preferred way of working. Now you want the entire team to follow the organizational standard. Imagine telling a unit nurse with 30 years of experience that the team developed a better way to perform baseline patient assessments. What do you think her response will be? Want an even greater challenge? Get a department of physicians to agree on a standard order set. I think you can understand the challenge of setting a common standard. The good news is that the work sequence will be developed and improved by the people who do the work. Yes, we want to follow evidence-based steps when a known standard exists, but all other activities will be standardized and tested by the team. The work sequence will be the final result of the improved work.

The final element of standard work is called "standard work in process." Some processes require small amounts of inventory to run. This occurs when one task step exceeds the takt time. To maintain an even flow, you must create a standard work in process (SWIP). SWIP is not a wildly varying number; it is calculated. You must monitor SWIP during operation to ensure it is being followed.

We begin by explaining why SWIP is needed. Assume we make wooden chairs. The workers in the process all have standard work and the work is balanced to the takt time. The operations are rough milling, sawing, finish milling, sanding, painting and finishing, assembly, and packing. Each operation has a 20-minute takt time and the standard work was written to meet the takt time. The unresolved issue is that the glue applied during assembly takes 60 minutes to dry.

In Chapter 2, we discussed the concept of continuous flow. For our chair assembly process, a chair must be completed every 20 minutes, but the gluing step takes 60 minutes. To pack one chair every 20 minutes, how many chairs do we need between assembly and packing? The answer is three. Every 20 minutes one chair is pulled for packing and every 20 minutes a chair is put into the queue from assembly. To maintain flow, we need three chairs' worth of standard work in process. The SWIP for this operation equals the C_t for gluing (60 minutes) divided by the T_t for the process (20 minutes): $SWIP = C_t/T_t = 60/20 = 3$ chairs.

In a healthcare example, emergency department patients arrive at a rate of four per hour for a takt time of 15 minutes (60 minutes ÷ 4 patients). We can balance the work in the ER (triage, registration, assessment, discharge), with each step taking less than the 15 minutes of takt time. However, the laboratory results take 60 minutes. How many patients of SWIP are needed to maintain one patient flow? In this case $C_t = 60$ minutes and the $T_t = 15$ minutes; the SWIP is $60 ÷ 15 = 4$. Regardless of the space needed to run the process, we must plan for an additional four places to accommodate the SWIP for the ER process. The tool used by Lean operations to document standard work is the standard work combination sheet (Figure 3.10).

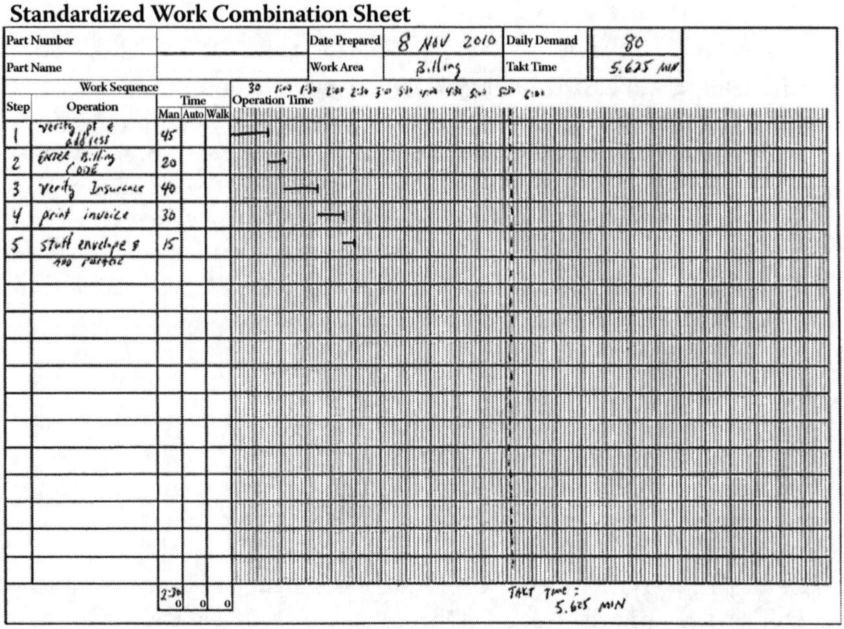

Standardized Work Combination Sheet

| Part Number | | | Date Prepared | 8 Nov 2010 | Daily Demand | 80 |
| Part Name | | | Work Area | Billing | Takt Time | 5.625 min |

Step	Operation	Man	Auto	Walk	Operation Time
1	verify pt & address	45			
2	Enter Billing code	20			
3	Verify Insurance	40			
4	print invoice	30			
5	stuff envelope & add postage	15			

2:30   0   0   0

TAKT TIME: 5.625 MIN

Figure 3.10   Standard work combination sheet.

You define Lean standard work by documenting the takt time, work sequence, and standard work in process. The Lean standard work tool is valuable because it allows you to audit the process to ensure that everyone follows the work standard. If work is not done to takt time or the outcomes vary, it is obvious that the standard work is not being followed or that waste is creeping back into the system. Standard work eliminates waste because it represents the documented institutional knowledge of how to complete the process in the easiest, safest, and best known way.

Process Control

The last tool that is commonly used to see and eliminate waste leverages the improvement principle of visual management. If you tried to improve a process, used several tools discussed previously to see and eliminate waste, and created a new standard encompassing takt time, work sequence, and standard work in process, you now need a way to manage the process to ensure that it continues to operate as designed. This is where process control comes in.

The official Lean term is "production control" and the tool used to manage production is the production control board. In healthcare, Lean practitioners

X-Ray Process Control Board			Date: 6/4/2010
Hour	*Plan*	*Actual*	*Comments*
0700–0800	3	3	No issues
0800–0900	3	2	Outpatient failed to show
0900–1000	3	3	No issues
1000–1100	3	1	Couldn't find O/P req, and isolation clean held up room
1100–1200	3	4	Simple ankle x-rays took less time than takt
1200–1300	3		
1300–1400	3		
1400–1500	3		
1500–1600	3		

Figure 3.11   Process control board.

generally substitute "process" for "production" because it better reflects the type of work. However the execution of the tool is identical for production and process, like all the universal tools we have discussed. A process control board can be used anywhere work is done. Figure 3.11 is an example.

A process control board has several requirements. The first is understanding takt time. A process control board documents completed units (output; patients in this case), but the units per hour are based on takt time. If we need to process three patients per hour, what is the takt time? In this example, 60 minutes ÷ 3 patients = 20 minutes. The "Plan" column always shows the units per hour to be completed based on takt time. The "Actual" column records the true number of patients completed within that hour. The takt time can change hourly, based on patient demand. The plan should change accordingly, to reflect changes in takt time.

A process control board also requires real time capture of actual output. The "Actual" column should be completed hourly by the people who do the work and reflect actual output. We are trying to see the difference between normal and abnormal. By capturing the plan versus the actual output, we can see abnormal at a glance. This is important because it makes the waste visible and allows us to intervene to get the work back on plan. It is important to note that seeing the waste is valuable only if someone does something about it.

The next item for a process control board is capturing sources of variation. The source of every variation from standard (good and bad) must be captured. These sources of variation are critical for future improvement and must be captured as they occur by the people who do the work. We can create a histogram of sources of variation. The leading causes of variation are candidates for future problems.

Let's review a common scenario. We were scheduled to perform x-ray examinations on 24 patients yesterday. In reality, we worked 1 hour of overtime and completed only 19 exams. We exceeded standard time by 1 hour and we missed the target by 5 patients—or nearly 20%. Can anyone explain what happened? If we are lucky and the same staff is scheduled, we may capture part of the data. More likely, the operation will absorb the variance and do better today.

Using a process control board, we can determine hour-by-hour activities. It may be possible to prevent the hour of overtime if we know by noon that we are three patients behind. We can capture the sources of variation to deliver valuable data for future problem solving. The key principle is to see normal and abnormal at a glance in order to take action.

After a week of variance reporting, the staff generates the chart shown in Figure 3.12. Which problem should we tackle first? Clearly the largest source of variation is that outpatients do not show up for their exams. This detail becomes a golden nugget that we can mine for further improvement. Here are a few suggestions for process control:

Frequency						
X						
X						
X						
X						
X						
X						
X						X
X			X		X
X	X		X		X
X	X	X	X	X	X
Outpatient failed to show	Isolation clean required	Wrong order	Order not signed	Patient got lost	Sending unit delay

Figure 3.12   Variance histogram.

1. Process control ties takt time and standard work together. The output of the process is based on customer demand (takt time). The work has been staffed appropriately; we used time observation and a loading diagram to eliminate waste and balance the work to takt time. The process control tool is used to manage visually (the fourth improvement principle) the adherence to standard work. If takt time is missed, waste has entered the system. We need to make the waste visible before we can do something about it.

2. Process control cannot be recreated after the fact; it must be managed in real time. Sources of variation must be captured in real time as well. Staff members, including physicians, have time to make entries on a process control board.

3. Entering information on a process control board should take less than 5 seconds. Determining variance from standard should take 5 seconds or less. If a board entry takes longer, the design is too complicated or the entries cannot be understood at a glance.

4. The board can be automated, but I do not recommend you start with automation. In capturing the data, the intent is to encourage adherence to standard work and capture sources of variation. These activities are difficult to automate. Also, the board and data are likely to change over time. Before you automate, take the time to understand clearly what you want.

5. This tool aims to manage process, not results. Results capture can be automated and analyzed after the fact, but process *must* be managed in real time.

6. Lean experts have found that staff will happily complete a board if management pays attention and uses the data. It is important to use the sources of variation (data captured) for further improvement. Having staff generate data that is not used is wasteful and disrespectful.

7. As a final tip, hold a shift-by-shift huddle in front of the process control board to review trending of performance, sources of variation, and what can be done to continue to eliminate waste. Encourage team members to participate in problem solving and idea generation.

Summary

Using these few simple tools, you can study and restudy a problem several times and gain repeated improvement. Each application of the tools is like peeling back the layers of an onion. Every layer reveals another layer. You may have to restudy a problem up to six times. Each application of the tools will reveal additional sources of waste. Until you remove some waste, other wastes remain hidden. You must solve some problems to expose others. This revelation is what separates good organizations from great organizations. Great organizations

Table 3.2 Seeing and Eliminating Waste

Tool	Helps See Waste	Helps Eliminate Waste
Takt time	X	
Direct observation	X	
Loading diagram	X	X
Spaghetti mapping	X	X
Circle diagram	X	X
Flow diagram	X	X
Value-added/non-value-added analysis	X	
Standard work		X
Process control	X	X

work to eliminate wastes that the good ones do not yet see. To conclude our discussion of tools, let's look at a final table. Remember that the most fundamental level of improvement is to see and eliminate waste. The tools we reviewed will help us do just that. Table 3.2 shows the tools and their functions (seeing waste, eliminating it, or both).

Putting Tools Together

We have discussed value-added and non-value-added activities. We reviewed the seven forms of waste and the five improvement principles for guiding our thinking when generating solutions to eliminate waste. We followed up with a detailed discussion of common tools used to see and eliminate waste. Great improvement leaders understand the tools and when to apply them. Not all wastes, principles, and tools apply to every situation. Also, these approaches are not usually meant to stand alone even though they can be used independently.

Typically, several wastes are identified using several tools. After that, a few improvement principles are chosen to generate a new solution that minimizes or eliminates non-value-added activity. The common team-based approaches that utilize the tools are A3 thinking, value stream mapping and analysis, and kaizen improvement. A3 thinking is embedded in both value stream mapping and kaizen improvement, so we will begin there.

A3 Theme:		Date:	Revision:
Reason for Improvement	Gap Analysis		Follow up Plans:
			Action Who When
Current Performance and Reflections on Current Performance:			
		Measurement Tracking	
	Countermeasure and Action Plans		
Target Performance:			
		Reflections	

Figure 3.13   A3 form.

A3 Thinking

Most improvement approaches follow the scientific method you learned in ninth grade biology. In healthcare, clinical trials and evidence-based practice are based on the scientific method of (1) developing a hypothesis, (2) testing the hypothesis, and (3) drawing conclusions. Improvement thus becomes an experiment in which new approaches are tested to determine whether an impact can be measured as a result of the new approach. Lean organizations use A3 thinking to implement the scientific method. Figure 3.13 is an A3 document. A3 thinking serves several purposes, but the key uses are:

- Problem solving and/or improvement
- Communication of problem solving and/or improvement activities
- Approval of resources or justification of use
- Committee work project management
- Documentation of strategy
- Lean improvement identified from a value stream map

Table 3.3   A3 Sections

Section	Content
Theme	Title of A3; brief description of problem to be studied
Reason for improvement	Three to five high level bullet points describing why improvement is necessary; when possible link benefits to customer and/or strategy of organization
Current conditions and reflections on current conditions	Define process as it currently exists (conditions such as volume, quantity, performance, time, quality, cost); reflections include perceptions of what works and does not work well
Target condition	What the future process should look like including both performance and culture; define clear measures and targets in this section
Gap analysis	Define what creates gap between current and target conditions; section may include wastes and their root or direct causes
Countermeasures and action plans	Document solutions to wastes defined in gap analysis; solutions can be tested in small controlled experiments; the testing plan is the action plan for this section; document result anticipated for each test of change
Follow-up plans	The what, who, and when actions that document changes; rollout plans are documented in this section
Measurement tracking	Charts reporting trends of outcome measures and targets identified in target condition section
Reflections	Documents organizational learning so that future teams can learn from this A3

Sections of the A3 also vary based on format, but the typical sections include the theme, current conditions, target conditions, gap analysis, countermeasures and action plans, follow-up plans, measurement tracking, and reflections. Table 3.3 shows contents of the A3 sections. Lean organizations use A3 thinking to guide the problem solving efforts of most of their team-based improvements. It is a great tool to integrate the application of tools so that waste can be seen and eliminated.

Value Stream Mapping and Analysis

W. Edwards Deming, a famous management quality consultant, said "It is not enough to do your best; you must know what to do, and then do your best."[*] Every operation presents countless opportunities to improve. Where do we begin? Value stream mapping and analysis provide the process and structure to identify what to do; from there you can improve and do your best. Value stream mapping (VSM) enables you to deliver an action plan for improvement. Also known as product and information flow mapping, VSM provides a structure and process that identify waste within a value stream, identify the sources of the waste, and develop a vision for the future and an action plan to deliver the future process.[†]

A value stream consists of all of the process activities required to deliver value to a customer. Beginning with the customer definition of value (remember the value-added versus non-value-added principles), the value stream covers all the tasks done to deliver value. A value stream typically begins with a customer need and ends when the need is met. Work normally spans many different departments; a value stream is *not* confined to one department.

For example, if a patient arrives for a pre-admission surgical consult, he or she will meet with registration, an OR nurse, and an anesthesiologist. He or she may also require laboratory tests and x-rays after discussing the procedure with a surgeon. At the end of the visit, the area is cleaned by environmental services and supplies are restocked. This work spans at least six departments. The value stream is broader than that of a single department.

Making an improvement in isolation (for example only in the OR department) will yield only marginal improvement. Improvement must occur across the entire value stream by engaging all departments to deliver value to the patient. In improving the value stream, waste is eliminated from the system—not moved from one department to another. Spot improvements may hold promise but rarely create revolutionary change. To complete a value stream mapping and analysis activity, you must accomplish the following high level activities:

1. Assemble a team with cross-functional representation across the value stream.
2. Determine measurable outcomes of the improvement based on the table categories below.

---

[*] http://thinkexist.com/quotes/w.edwardsdeming/ ThinkExist.com Quotations, 1999–2010.
[†] Rother, M. and Shook, J. 1998. *Learning to See*. Lean Enterprise Institute, Brookline, MA, p. 4.

Area of Focus	Outcome Measure
Morale	Measuring staff engagement, team morale, or human development
Quality	Process quality or clinical quality outcome
Delivery	Measures of on-time performance, lead times, or wait times
Cost	Measures of productivity or cost per unit of output
Volume	Measure of growth in demand for services

3. Specify value from the customer perspective.
4. Determine the beginning and ending points of the value stream.
5. Process map current (the real as-is) process (Figure 3.14).
6. Capture data on current process; add data for each process step (Table 3.4).
7. Identify waste in current process (Figure 3.15).
8. Analyze current state and summarize performance (Table 3.5). From this data summary example can you identify waste? Why are there so many non-value-added steps? Why does the process require 20+ hand-offs of information? What causes so much waiting between steps? Why is the reliability of the process so low? No matter how you see your process, the summary of the current state is what your customer actually sees!
9. Develop a future state process using the Lean improvement principles to guide thinking. Figure 3.16 is a sample future state map.
10. Perform a gap analysis between the current and future states to identify the specific projects needed to realize the future state.
11. Prioritize the projects identified in the gap analysis based on an assessment of their impacts on goals and efforts to implement (Figure 3.17).
12. Sequence improvements on a timeline (Figure 3.18).
13. Document the improvement plan in detail by completing the first three sections of an A3 form for each project identified.

The key deliverables from the value stream mapping and analysis activity are the future state vision, the detailed improvement plan, and the measures of success. The future state map creates the vision for the team that reveals what the new process will look like across the entire value stream. The detailed action plan lists the specific projects that will be completed to transform the value stream from the current state to the future state. These projects include kaizen activity

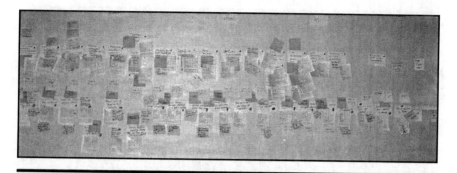

Figure 3.14   Current process state map.

Table 3.4   Data Captured for Tasks

Measurement	Definition
Step name	Document name of task
Begins with	Document what initiates activity
Ends with	Document what ends activity
Task lead time	Calendar (clock) time from *begins with* to *ends with* for this task
Manual touch time	Actual hands-on time for completing task (includes walking, writing, talking on the phone, and performing task)
Items in queue	Number of identical tasks sitting in the in-box at this specific time
Process quality %	Percentage of times the task can be completed without need to check , clarify, or repeat the activity

(discussed next) and quick wins that will create flow and pull, eliminate defects, and enable visual management of the entire value stream. It is important to note that nothing changes as a result of value stream analysis. Remember W.E Deming's wisdom from the beginning of the chapter. Now that you know what to do, you can do your best!

A value stream mapping and analysis event typically requires a cross-functional team of 12 to 15 members. It is important that both line staff and management participate in sessions. If the focus is clinical, it is mandatory to have physician input as well. The activity can take 2 to 5 days, depending on the

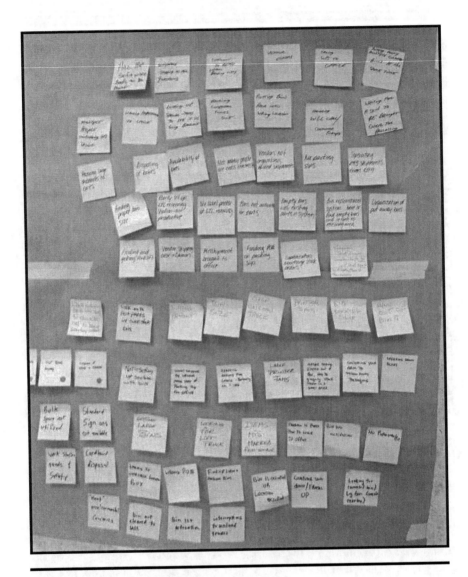

Figure 3.15 Wastes identified in current state.

scope of the value stream; in healthcare, 2.5 to 3 days are usually required. Sessions should run on consecutive days to enable the team to maintain the continuity that delivers a better end product. Additionally, the activities build on one another so consecutive sessions improve linkage from one activity to the next, making the process easier for the team.

Table 3.5 Data Summary

Measure	Ambulatory	Subacute
Number of steps	35	68
Value-added steps	5	4
Non-value-added steps	30	64
Value-added %	14	6
Lead time (min)	217	1423
Manual touch time (min)	52	231
Number of hand-offs	17	26
Items in queue	385	53
Process quality %	0.0494	0.00195
Demand or volume	41,600 patients annually	

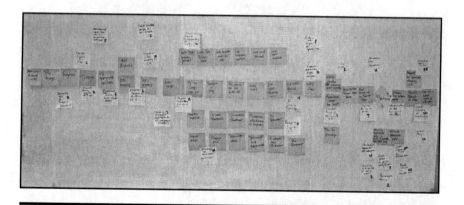

Figure 3.16   Future state map. (Courtesy of Lakeridge Health. With permission.)

Kaizen

Now that you have an action plan, it is time to deliver results. One tool that helps deliver results while simultaneously changing the culture of your organization is an approach known as a kaizen event, also known as practical kaizen training, kaizen blitz, rapid improvement event, or kaizen workshop, all based on the same principles. A kaizen event follows A3 thinking to improve part of a value stream, and typically involves six to ten team members. An event typically

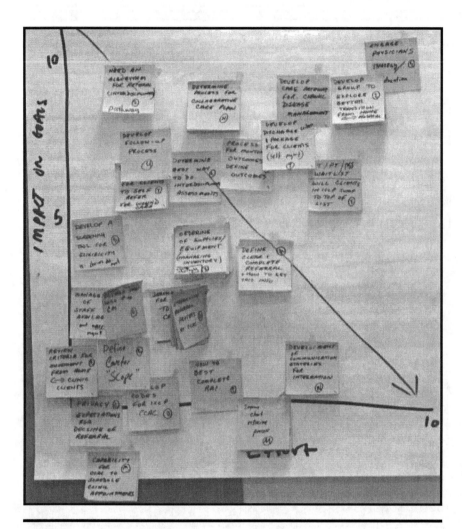

Figure 3.17   Prioritizing projects.

takes 2 to 5 days to complete, depending on the scope of the problem to be solved. The amount of time does not matter. The important issue is that all the A3 thinking must be completed with the correct level of detail, discipline, and integrity. Table 3.6 is a standard agenda.

A kaizen event actually begins several weeks before the actual improvement activities. Measures and targets are selected. Baseline data is collected on these measures. Appropriate improvement team members are selected. Support logistics and supplies are prepared to ensure that the team can operate with minimal barriers.

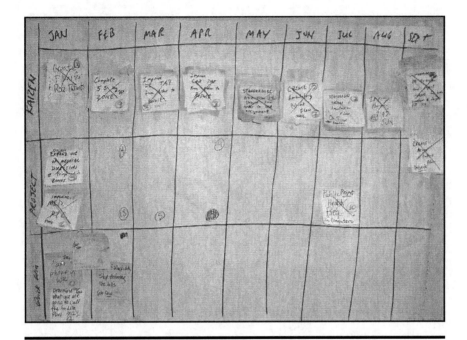

Figure 3.18   Sequence of improvement.

Table 3.6   Kaizen Event Daily Agenda

Day 1: Define current conditions (see waste)	Day 2: Develop solutions (eliminate waste)	Day 3: Implement and test solutions	Day 4: Document new standard work
Team training; review measures and targets; use appropriate tools to see waste; gather time observation data; name 50 to 100 forms of waste	Prioritize wastes; develop counter-measures and action plans to eliminate waste; use Lean principles to design new work flow	Implement countermeasures; train team members on new process; verify effectiveness of solutions by measuring	Standardize work; document standard work; document event results; deliver presentation; recognize team

The week of the kaizen event is followed by an intense "sustaining period" during which all affected team members are trained to the new standard work. Visual management systems are monitored hourly to ensure that the new standard is followed, the correct results are delivered, and no unintended consequences are uncovered. New problems that arise are solved immediately and communicated to the team. The case studies in Chapter 4 examine actual kaizen activities in detail and highlight the corresponding results. The key benefits of kaizen include:

1. Identification of the correct team members to solve a problem
2. Selection of focused, key improvement measures
3. Removal of organizational barriers to enable the team to make rapid change
4. Ability of the team to move quickly through the team cycles of forming, storming, norming, and performing
5. Compression of the timeline to see results
6. Transfer of improvement knowledge as team members learn to see and eliminate waste by doing
7. Improvement based on a more strategic value stream plan and eliminating the spot improvement phenomenon

As we conclude this section, I'd like to emphasize the importance of kaizen activity. In all my years of studying Lean improvement, I have never seen an organization transform without kaizen activity. Of course, other approaches to improvement and project-based approaches can and do generate amazing results as well. But if you want to change your culture to one in which everyone sees and eliminates waste, you must routinely practice kaizen. I have never seen organizations succeed (successfully transform their cultures) otherwise.

5S

Earlier in this chapter, we talked about visual management as one of the Lean principles. Visual management allows everyone to see, know, and understand. One of the best ways to begin improvement and to start to build discipline in your organization is to implement a rigorous 5S program. 5S is a management system based on a visually managed workplace that creates a high performing work area. The system is called 5S because the key elements are five Japanese words that begin with *S*. Table 3.7 lists the 5Ss and their loose translations. When implementing 5S, management should select an area of focus such as a nursing station, rehab treatment room, or scheduling office. Implementation involves the following tasks:

Table 3.7   5S Definitions

Japanese Word	Loose English Translation of Principle
Seiri	Sort and remove unnecessary items from workplace
Seiton	Set in order: organize remaining items to promote standard workflow and enable standardized work
Seiso	Shine: return workplace to like-new conditions
Seiketsu	Standardize: create standardized consistent work practices
Shitsuke	Sustain personal discipline to maintain previous 4S principles

1. Remove unnecessary items from the work place. Create an area to consolidate such materials, supplies, and equipment so that they may be redistributed, returned to stock, recycled, or sold. Some items will need to be scrapped including obsolete wall signs.
2. After unnecessary items have been removed, thoroughly clean the area. Mop, dust, paint, repair the walls, repair broken equipment, and wax the floors. This activity will return the area to like-new conditions. Be sure to address all safety issues including fire extinguishers, fire exits, sharps containers, electrical cords, oxygen and suction connections, hand hygiene dispensers, etc. Repair missing and damaged molding, floors, and cabinets. Address broken items in the clinical areas including blood pressure cuffs, beds, chairs, stretchers, etc.
3. Map workflows and reorganize the necessary materials, supplies, and equipment in a way that enables proper workflow and standard work. When items are returned, assign a home position and identifier to every item. The home position should be both obvious and intuitive. Missing or misplaced items should be obvious at a glance.
4. Create standard operating procedures to maintain the work area. The procedures should cover restocking, cleaning, and organizing schedules for *all* employees who work in the area. These procedures should be visible to everyone and whether they are or are not followed correctly should be immediately obvious.
5. Develop a sustaining system that includes cascading audits by employees and management. The audit system should cover all of previous 4S activities to ensure that the organization maintains the integrity of the four principles. Take action to maintain and improve the system.

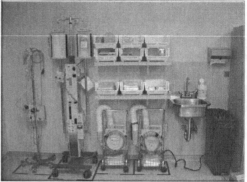

Figure 3.19 Before and after picture of 5S improvement in an emergency department resuscitation room. (From Credit Valley Hospital, Mississauga, Ontario, Canada. With permission.)

Fortunately, 5S is a well-documented tool. With a quick search on the Internet, you can drill down and research 5S activity based on areas of specialization including ED, OR, laboratory, administration, diagnostic imaging, finance, and IT. The 5S system allows staff to determine what is needed, where it is needed, and in what quantities; this creates staff buy-in. A robust 5S system will eliminate the waste of hunting, searching, and gathering, and thus positively impact staff and provider satisfaction, patient safety, lead times for services, and productivity. The simple act of looking for lost items wastes a lot of staff time.

5S incorporates the common tools discussed earlier because it uses spaghetti mapping and process mapping to help see and eliminate waste. The system is managed visually, enabling everyone to discern normal from abnormal at a glance. When combined with the real-time actions taken by management and staff to return an abnormal condition to normal, a robust 5S system will make a significant difference in the day-to-day operations of a workplace. As an example, Figure 3.19 illustrates emergency department performance before and after 5S improvement.

Along with eliminating waste, I recommend that organizations start their improvement with 5S activity because it instills a sense of discipline within a team. This discipline is essential if we expect staff to follow standard work consistently as improvement continues. If a staff member does not consistently return a piece of equipment back to its home after using it, how will he or she consistently follow all the steps in a complex clinical pathway? By practicing 5S, staff members gain valuable experience in improvement methods and build on their success.

Chapter 4

Case Studies

We have covered some of the theory behind the science of Lean improvement and discussed the value-added and non-value-added principles. We talked about the seven wastes: overproduction, overprocessing, waiting, inventory, defects, motion, and transportation. These wastes constitute most non-value-added activities. We also reviewed the principles of improvement: flow, pull, defect-free, visual management, and kaizen. These principles help eliminate large amounts of non-value added activities.

Several common tools are used to help Lean practitioners see and eliminate waste. These common tools can be used many times to restudy the same process, each time exposing additional layers of waste. The tools can be used as stand-alone aids or may be applied via a value stream analysis or kaizen event to systematically see and eliminate the waste while changing the culture of an organization. Let's now review how the application of Lean has been used in healthcare to improve access, improve clinical and service quality, reduce costs, and improve staff and medical staff morale.

Revolutionizing Emergency Services: Enhanced Quality and Access

In the acute care setting, the overall performance of a hospital organization is reflected by its emergency department performance. In Chapter 1, we talked about the current state of emergency departments across North America and the challenges they face in providing access to services. Visits to local emergency

Table 4.1 Measurable Outcomes

True North Measure Dimension	Measure
Clinical quality	Reduce left-without-being-seen rate by 50%
Service quality	Increase patient satisfaction survey scores by 10% absolute
Access	Reduce emergency department length-of-stay (LOS) stratified by triage score by 40%

rooms for treatment of minor injuries typically lead to 4- or 5-hour waits—a telling commentary on the overall performance of today's healthcare organizations. To see how positive change is possible, let's look at a case study of an emergency department that successfully applied Lean to improve access and quality.

Every year, about 34,000 patients visit the emergency department at Valleyview Hospital. The improvement process began with a value stream analysis to see the waste in the current state and develop plans for improvement. Before value stream mapping, management must define the measurable outcomes for a project. For this department, the measures and targets shown in Table 4.1 were chosen. The improvement team conducted a 3-day value stream analysis that led to the improvement plan shown in Table 4.2

Let's review the execution of a kaizen event. In this case, the team prioritized the improvement plans and decided to begin with a kaizen event focused on reducing the lengths of stays in the emergency department, specifically for medium acuity patients. These patients accounted for 33% of the volume through the department. The team was most concerned about the left-without-being-seen (LWBS) rate among medium acuity patients that exceeded 6%. Of the 11,200 patients in this triage category each year, 6% or 673 of them arrived at the emergency room and left the hospital without seeing a physician.

Note that the specific kaizen improvement targets of a 40% reduction in length of stay and a 50% reduction in LWBS are aligned directly with the value stream measurable outcomes. As a rule, we do not want to start improvement on goals that are not directly aligned strategically to bigger picture goals. Table 4.3 shows the targets for the improvement activities. At Valleyview Hospital, the improvement team met and analyzed current conditions. They identified the wastes and root causes shown in Table 4.4, then developed countermeasures for the wastes observed. They tested changes to see whether their countermeasures were effective. The countermeasures implemented are listed in Table 4.5.

A calculation of takt time showed that five patient spaces were needed to perform this process effectively. The five spaces refer to the additional beds needed

Table 4.2   Improvement Plan

Type of Improvement	Action
Quick win	Determine standard process for patients returning from diagnostic imaging
Quick win	Install phone with direct access to taxi company in waiting room
Project	Improve consultant response time
Project	Expand use of appropriate medical directives
Project	Finalize and implement medicine reconciliation practices
Kaizen	Create ambulatory patient flow
Kaizen	Create medium acuity patient flow
Kaizen	Create acute patient flow
Kaizen	Improve diagnostic imaging turn-around time (order to results available)
Kaizen	Improve pharmacy turn-around time (from order of medicine to dispensing)
Kaizen	Implement 5S system for equipment and supplies
Kaizen	Standardize patient transfer and report process for internal and external transfers
Kaizen	Standardize admission process from order to admit to bed assignment
Kaizen	Create standard work for triage and registration patient flow

for patients waiting for diagnostic results to return. A small treatment room was converted to a waiting area for patients awaiting results. The cycle time/takt time bar chart (Figure 4.1) showed that one nurse could manage the workload and only a portion of a physician's time would be needed. This was important information, because a single physician currently covered the entire department for a large part of each day. The organization originally assumed (as I find at many organizations) that additional physician working hours were needed to impact access and quality of care.

Table 4.3   Kaizen Targets and Measures

Dimension	Measure	Baseline	Target
Access	Average length of stay (ALOS)	4.9 hours	Reduce by 40% to 2.94 hours
Quality	Left-without-being-seen (LWBS) by physician percentage	6%	3%

Table 4.4   Wastes and Root Causes

Key Waste	Root Causes
Lack of direction for patients entering emergency department	Unclear signage; queue system not consistently effective
Medical directives not started in timely manner	Layout not conducive to initiating directives; no standard in place for initiating
Time lost looking for forms	Forms not available on demand
Delay in registration	Trigger to begin not consistent; waiting designed between triage and registration
Lost nurse productivity	Poor work space layout of equipment, medications, and supplies; no consistent work practice
Communication waste with ancillary services	Inconsistent triggers for action
Delays in MD/RN responses	No standard triggers
Waiting for room to be cleaned	Lack of clear and consistent triggers

Next, the improvement team needed to determine when to trigger the physician to go to the newly designed area. Walking to the area too frequently would result in a productivity loss caused by excess motion. Infrequent walking would delay patient care and lead to excessive waiting. The team and medical staff agreed that a combination of three physician activities would serve as the trigger. Any combination of patients waiting to be seen, patients waiting for reassessment, or patients waiting for treatment would count toward a total of

Table 4.5   Countermeasures

Key Wastes	Root Causes	Countermeasures
Lack of direction for patients entering emergency department	Unclear signage; queuing system not consistently effective	Improve signage; develop patient queue system
Medical directives not started in timely manner	Layout not conducive to initiating directives; no standard in place to initiate directives	Reorganize work-space to accommodate starting medical directives; create common standard for initiating directive
Time lost looking for forms	Forms not available on demand	Auto print forms or add icons to print on demand
Delay in registration	Trigger to begin not consistent; delay between triage and registration	Create standard work with triggers; directly link triage to registration
Lost nurse productivity	Work space layout of equipment, medications, and supplies; no consistent work practice	Locate supplies and equipment at point of use; develop standard work practices
Communication waste with ancillary services	Inconsistent triggers for action	Develop standard triggers
Delays in MD/RN responses	No standard triggers for action	Develop standard triggers
Waiting for room to be cleaned	Lack of clear and consistent triggers	Develop standard triggers

three activities. When the count of three was met, a nurse would travel a short distance (fewer than 30 steps) and inform the physician that the trigger had been met. When the physician finished with a patient, he or she would go to the medium acuity area where patients already were prepared, thus optimizing physician time.

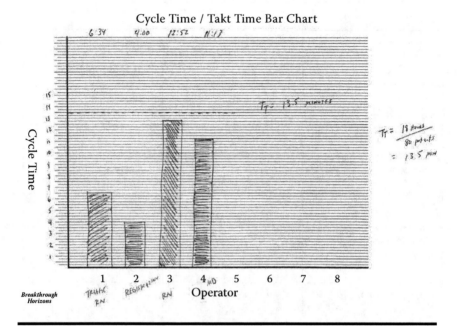

Figure 4.1   Cycle time/takt time bar chart.

Table 4.6   Results of ER Kaizen

Dimension	Measure	Baseline	Reduction Target	Actual[a]	Change
Access	ALOS	4.9 hours	40%	3.36 hours	31.4% reduction
Quality	LWBS	6%	50%	0.79%	85% reduction

ALOS = average length of stay. LWBS = left without being seen [by physician].
[a] N = 500 patients.

Visual management systems were put in place and 5S activities were performed for room set-up and supply organization; process control was established. Each patient was tracked against the target visit time (slightly shorter than 3 hours). Whenever a patient's length of visit exceeded 3 hours, the reason for the length of stay was identified at the time of discharge from the department. All staff including administrative and medical personnel were trained to follow the new process. The results from the kaizen activity at Valleyview Hospital were dramatic. Improvements were realized in both visit time and LWBS. Both administrative staff and medical staff satisfaction increased and patients were pleased with the changes. Table 4.6 summarizes the results.

As noted earlier, quality and patient safety always come first in healthcare settings. With these criteria in mind, improvement in the LWBS rate was the most impressive aspect of Valleyview's success. At this improved run rate, fewer than 50 patients will leave without receiving care each year, compared to 673 patients before Lean improvements were made!

No matter how good or how poor your hospital's current performance, I believe it is possible to realize the same rate of improvement in your emergency department. Keep in mind that the impressive results at Valleyview were achieved after a single kaizen event followed by an intense sustaining period. I must note that the management team was highly committed to the success of this project and did an amazing job with the sustaining activities.

Accelerating Productivity and Access in Diagnostic Imaging

We will now focus on another key area of concern in healthcare today: diagnostic imaging (DI). Several modalities fall under this broad field: x-ray, ultrasound, computed tomography (CT) scanning, and magnetic resonance imaging (MRI). These procedures provide important images of body anatomy that allow accurate diagnosis of illness.

In terms of healthcare improvement, DI procedures often attract a great deal of attention for two reasons: access and cost. DI procedures can be expensive, leading to questions about whether they are necessary. (Such questions might not arise if DI procedures were inexpensive; but all unnecessary examinations are wasteful.) According to Lean methodology, an examination performed in excess of value is an overprocessing waste. In other words, concerns based on cost are not completely unfounded. However, if evidence-based guidelines are always used to determine the need for diagnostic tests, DI procedures should always provide value to customers.

A more pressing concern is access. Acute care DI is bombarded with emergency department, inpatient, and outpatient orders. A lot of time is spent prioritizing exam urgencies and reading results. (Reminder: prioritizing tasks add no value to patients.) During booking, clarifying the order, looking for results, and waiting for the patient to be transported to and from the exam room, many phone calls are exchanged between the ordering department and DI.

Additionally, DI equipment is expensive. Capital is required to purchase the equipment and also to provide a special room to house it. Maintenance costs are high and the IT systems required to provide the digital output are expensive as well. Finally, a highly educated staff is needed to run a DI department. Skilled technologists are required to conduct the examinations, radiologists are needed

Table 4.7　Measurable MRI Outcomes

True North Measure Dimension	Measure
Process quality	Reduce number of incomplete order requisitions by 80%
Service quality	Increase patient satisfaction survey scores by 10% absolute
Access	Reduce wait times to less than 2 weeks; reduce cancelled patients from 6 to 1 per day
Cost	Reduce labor costs per exam by 25%

to read the results, and well-trained scheduling, billing, and coding personnel are needed to manage the complex array of procedures and codes. Exams that are carried out incorrectly impose significant health risks to staff and patients. Staff and patient exposure to x-rays, and MRI technology, which is a risk to patients with certain types of implants, must be monitored closely. Finally, heavy demand requires effective equipment utilization to enable timely patient access.

In this case study, we visit Wellbeing Healthcare Center. (Like the Valleyview case study, this fictionalized account is based on an actual North American hospital.) The Wellbeing site hosts two MRI machines and is part of a large urban teaching hospital in a downtown location. Both imaging machines run 16 hours a day. Each machine has a team of two technologists. The control room typically houses four people (more if a radiologist is present). As always, we began Lean improvement with a value stream analysis. The key measures are detailed in Table 4.7.

The results of the value stream analysis delivered an improvement plan that included six months of kaizen event activity and two projects. One of the kaizen events involved developing standard work for the MRI technologists. For this pair of MRI scanners, the demand was 75 referrals per day. Each machine had a capacity of 30 exams over two shifts per day, totaling 60 exams per day—significantly below the 75 patient referral demand. As a result, the department reported a backlog of more than 3 weeks.

As we know, the starting point for Lean is calculating takt time. In this case, we first calculated the available time for MRI scanning. The machines were available 16 hours per day multiplied by 60 minutes for a total of 960 minutes available for work. They were available continuously throughout the two shifts, even during staggered breaks and lunch times for staff. The volume was 75 referrals per day, thus the takt time was 960 minutes ÷ 75 exams = 12.8 minutes.

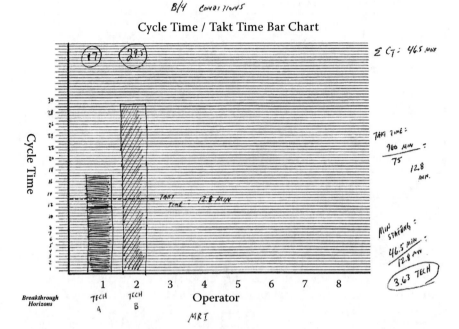

Figure 4.2 MRI loading.

Next, the improvement team analyzed the manual cycle times for the two technicians. Recall that the manual cycle time is the actual work of the people who do it. One technician was responsible for preparing patients: ensuring they were dressed appropriately (or helping them change), reviewing the safety checklist, starting the IV/oral contrast if required, and changing the room over from one exam to the next. The second technician confirmed the exams in the system, entered the appropriate information, and performed the examinations. The cycle time/takt time loading diagram looked like Figure 4.2.

As the improvement team analyzed the manual cycle times for the MRI technologists, they encountered a challenge. Each examination (depending on the body part to be examined) revealed a different cycle time. The solution was to calculate weighted average manual cycle times based on the type of exam. Table 4.8 shows how the calculations were made. The weighted average is the sum of the weighted minutes or 29.5 minutes.

Next, a calculation was made to determine the minimum staffing required. In this case the minimum staffing was the sum of the manual cycle time (17 minutes + 29.5 minutes) divided by the takt time (12.8 minutes) or 17 minutes +

Table 4.8 Weighted Average Manual Cycle time

Examination Type	Examinations/Day (Total = 60)	% of Total	Cycle Time (Ct) in Minutes	Weighted Minutes (% × Ct)
Head	12	20	30	6 minutes
Extremity (simple)	18	40	20	8 minutes
Extremity (complex)	15	25	35	8.75 minutes
Abdomen	15	15	45	6.75 minutes

Total Weighted Average Manual Cycle Time = 29.5 minutes

29.5 minutes ÷ 12.8 = 46.5 ÷12.8 or 3.63 technologists. Assuming that no wastes would be removed, 3.63 technologists were required for the MRI department at Wellness Healthcare to handle its current volume of referrals. However, in virtually any scenario, wastes can be identified and eliminated. Table 4.9 reveals the key wastes identified.

The team quickly identified solutions to eliminate the key wastes. To prompt patients to change clothes independently and correctly, better instructions were given to them before their exams and better signage was added to the waiting area. To address the claustrophobia problem, a wooden closet simulating the MRI scanner was built. Patients were asked to step inside the enclosure to simulate the feeling of an MRI. Although the simulation did not eliminate all cancellations from claustrophobic patients, it reduced them by about 75%!

Eliminating the double-check of the safety checklist proved more challenging because no operation ever wants to sacrifice patient safety. In this case, the team found that the double-check was often carried out not because of actual risk, but because the technologist performing the exam did not trust the preparing technologist. The team decided to perform an FMEA (Failure Mode Effects Analysis) to assess the risk. Double-checking was encouraged for higher risk patients, but redundancy due to mistrust was dramatically reduced.

Finally, 5S activity (sort, set in order, shine, standardize, and sustain) was performed and enabled IVs to be started closer to the point of use. This eliminated the waste of hunting and gathering supplies and equipment by the IV nurse. After all the changes were put in place, new standard work was written for the preparation technologist and the exam technologist. A new loading diagram was also created (Figure 4.3).

Table 4.9   Key Wastes

Waste	Frequency (%)	Time Lost (Minutes)	Weighted Minutes
Patient not dressed properly; had to change into gown	80	5	4
Claustrophic patient; cancelled appointment	5	44.5	2.2
Technologist double-checked safety checklist before beginning exam	100	3	3
IV supplies and IV nurse not ready; exam delayed	10	15	1.5

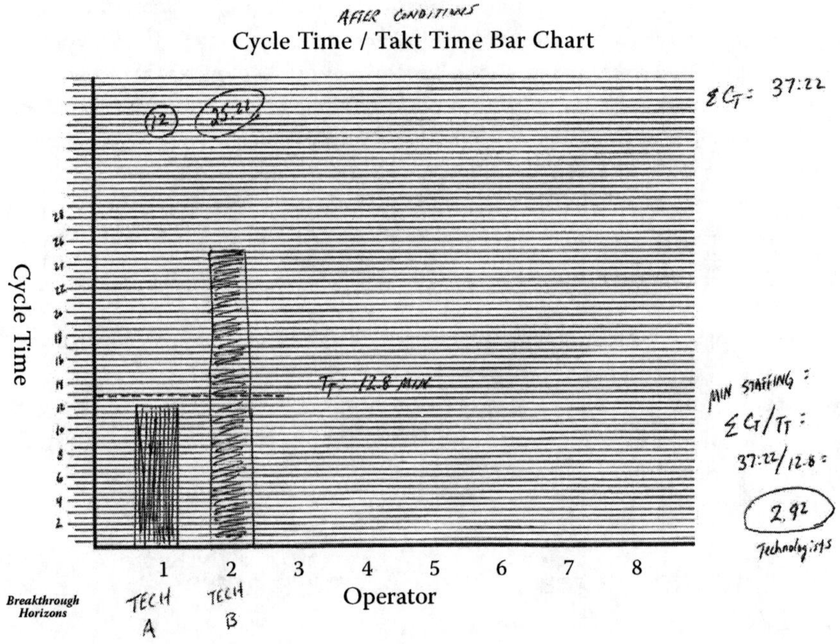

Figure 4.3   New MRI loading.

Table 4.10 MRI Results

Dimension	Measure	Baseline	Target	Actual	% Change
Quality	Complete referral	44%	80%	82%	86% increase
Access	Wait time	24 days	14 days	8 days	67% reduction
Access	Cancellation	6/day	1/day	1.7 day	72% reduction
Cost/ productivity	Technologist hours/exam	1.07	0.80	0.65	39% reduction
Growth	Volume	60/day	72/day	74/day	23% increase

The loading diagram showed another important finding. As a result of eliminating waste, the minimum staffing calculation changed dramatically. The new calculation was $(37.37) \div 12.8 = 2.92$ technologists. This means that process could now run with three technologists instead of four! Management redeployed the fourth technologist who filled an open requisition for a budgeted new position.

A few other value stream improvements were made over the next 6 months. The slot times were adjusted to represent the actual exam times. The scheduling department added four examinations per day by booking appointments according to these new times. A rapid fill process was put in place to capture missed and/or cancelled appointments. Significant improvements were made on the requisition order; this saved many hours of time in the scheduling department and the control room. Radiologists standardized their protocols. This allowed the process to run based on department standards and not personality-based (radiologist-specific) standards. The net results of the changes are shown in Table 4.10.

Such opportunities may exist in your diagnostic imaging department. Regardless of performance level, practicing kaizen will make it better. Using the tools, techniques, and applications of Lean thinking in your hospital's processes will allow you to discover hidden capacity, improve patient and staff safety, increase access, and improve your cost position.

Creating the Ultimate Patient Experience: A Visit to an Orthopedic Clinic

You have probably waited in a physician's office and noticed the high number of patients sitting in the waiting room. You may have wondered whether the physicians ever get a break! Do they take lunch or even pause for a moment to

Table 4.11 Key Measures for Orthopedic Clinic

Measure	Baseline	Target
Access: new patients seen within 14 calendar days	48%	74%
Growth: meet budgeted patient volumes	Under budget by 10%	Exceed budget by 10%
Patient satisfaction: visit length	3.1 hours	1.5 hours

collect their thoughts? When 20 or more people are queued in a waiting room, a break doesn't seem likely. A 3-hour clinic visit is not an ultimate patient experience.

This case study looks at patient experience during a visit to an orthopedic clinic at a large urban, teaching hospital we'll call City General. The orthopedic clinic is very large: 18 physicians treat patients. To begin the improvement process, the team undertook a value stream analysis after management identified key goals for improvement (Table 4.11). The improvement plan from the value stream analysis yielded the following kaizen opportunities:

■ Create patient flow for clinic.
■ Create standard work for x-ray technicians, clerical functions (check-in and out at front desk), nursing, technicians, and physicians.
■ Create standard work for scheduling call center and level clinic schedule.

The improvement began with a series of standard work kaizen events. A series of kaizen activities was conducted to eliminate waste and create and balance standard work to the takt time of the process. Let's look at the standard work event for the x-ray process at the clinic.

Most patients who came to the orthopedic clinic had x-rays. Some were examined while wearing their casts and others had their casts removed for the examination. Cast removal was the decision of the physician. When the improvement process began, no clear standards were in place to determine whether an x-ray should take place before or after cast removal. Creating clear standards was an important first step. The improvement team also discovered that although the x-ray technologists usually ran ahead of takt time, the physicians (as many as eight at any time) constantly complained that they had no patients to see. How was this possible? To understand the problem, the improvement team took a closer look.

They discovered that all physicians independently set up appointment times for their patients and used completely different systems. For example, one doctor would schedule 10 patients to come in at 9:00 a.m.; another would schedule patients every 20 minutes. In fact, each physician followed a different scheduling pattern. X-rays were handled on a first-in-first-out basis, so if five of Physician A's patients appeared before Physician B's first patient arrived, they were x-rayed first. As a result, too many of Physician A's patients were x-rayed too early, creating a waste of overproduction. Meanwhile, while x-rayed patients waited to see Physician A, Physicians B, C, D … were all waiting for patients (and fuming).

When improvements began at City General, plans existed to increase x-ray capacity by adding two machines and more rooms for the physicians. The thinking (incorrect as it was) was that adding x-ray equipment and personnel, as well as more rooms where patients could be staged, physician wait times would be reduced and more volume would move through the clinic. However, by using Lean thinking, the improvement team realized that increased capacity would solve the *wrong* problem. The correct solution was to level the x-ray work to meet the needs of all the physicians holding clinic hours.

Another important Lean tool that proved helpful at City General was the heijunka board. *Heijunka* loosely translates to "production leveling" or "production smoothing." The orthopedic clinic wanted an even flow of x-ray patients to physicians. The improvement team created the heijunka board in Figure 4.4. According to the board, the new system steps were:

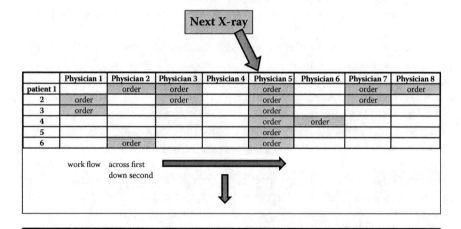

Figure 4.4 X-ray leveling. (From SRHC Navigator Kaizen event report. With permission.)

1. Place x-ray forms in order by physician in order of patient arrival.
2. Following the signal (Velcro-applied arrow) for the next patient, perform an x-ray on a patient for Physician 5, then proceed left to right (to Physicians 6 and 7) until you get to Physician 8 to implement leveling.
3. After reaching Physician 8, return to Physician 1 and complete an x-ray for each physician's patients in turn.
4. If a slot is empty (no x-ray patients waiting for the physician next in queue), skip the physician and go to the next open slot.
5. If all physician slots except one are empty, perform the x-rays top to bottom.
6. After two patients have completed their x-rays and are in queue waiting to be seen by the same physician, skip x-raying that physician's patients until one of the two patients goes to a treatment room; this prevents overprocessing.

This leveled workflow ensured that patients were available for all the physicians. Standard work was created for the x-ray technologists to ensure that their work time (cycle time) could be completed within the takt time. Standard work covered preparing patients, setting up the equipment, patient positioning, and conducting exams. The standard work and leveling combined to make the physician waits for patients virtually disappear. This improvement had a significant positive impact on provider satisfaction but, more importantly, it eliminated the demand for additional equipment. City General saved significant capital equipment costs.

Standard work was then created for the other clinic functions: scheduling, registration, nurses, orthopedic technicians, and physicians. Following the completion of standard work for all functions, the final step was to level the clinic visit times. Physician schedules were restructured to represent their actual lengths of both new and follow-up visits. These schedule changes were loaded into the master schedule and appointments were filled through a scheduling call center. The new level schedule created more volume in the clinic and the reduced wait time resulted in fewer appointment cancellations. Some physicians moved their clinic hours to different days of the week to create better clinic flow by leveling the patient volumes evenly across the work week. The net results of the changes are shown in Table 4.12.

You might note that the team did not hit its target for access. The goal was to see 75% of new patients within 14 days; the team achieved goal only 63% of the time. Is this a failure? Far from it. First, note that the new number represents a 31% improvement over baseline! Second, remember that teams don't always hit their goals. To meet the access target, we must restudy the problem and eliminate more waste from the system. In the spirit of continuous improvement, there is more to be done!

Table 4.12 Results of Value Stream Improvement at Orthopedic Clinic

Measure	Baseline	Target	Actual	% Change
Access: new patients seen within 14 calendar days	48%	75%	63%	31% increase
Growth: meeting budgeted patient volumes	Under budget by 10%	Exceed budget by 10%	Exceeded budget by 13%	N/A
Patient satisfaction: visit length	3.1 hours	1.5 hours	54 minutes	71% decrease

The difference in the performance of this clinic after Lean improvement was impressive. The changes occurred without impacting staffing and required no IT or capital improvement. The only change was elimination of non-value-added activity, resulting in improved quality, access, and cost. Patient appointment time was reduced by 2 hours; this meant less time away from work and reduced parking fees. Every clinic can be improved, so for the sake of your patients, I hope you experience the same rates of improvement at your organization. City General took a great step forward in creating the ultimate patient experience.

World Class Care at Inpatient Medical Unit

When the acuity of a patient exceeds emergency and clinic service capabilities, he or she must be admitted to a hospital. The general inpatient population can consume a large share of overall hospital resources second only to some surgical and intensive care patients. Medical unit patients often require interdisciplinary healthcare and a wide range of support provided by laboratory, pharmaceutical, therapeutic, and diagnostic services. Inpatient units are supported by biomedical staff, environmental services, and nutrition services. All these functions must work in harmony to create a healing environment following evidence-based practices for good outcomes.

Our next case study takes place at a large, community hospital we'll call St. Xavier Healthcare System. This hospital supports over 500 inpatient beds, provides a wide range of healthcare services including specialized cardiac care and oncology, and serves as a regional center for stroke care. These services and others are offered in addition to the general internal medicine capabilities that will serve as the focus of our discussion.

Table 4.13 Key Measures for Internal Medicine Value Stream

Measure	Baseline	Target
Access: reduce average length of stay	7.6 days	6.6 days
Quality: consistent treatment using evidence-based care	32%	90%
Quality: readmission rate within 30 days of discharge	8.3%	3%
Service quality: overall survey score	72%	85%

Improvement begins with selecting key measures and performing value stream analysis. The key measures for the internal medicine unit at St. Xavier are detailed in Table 4.13. The improvement plan that resulted from the value stream analysis led to many meaningful opportunities (Table 4.14). (Note: When you work within an inpatient value stream, completing all the improvement activities is a multi-year effort.)

Note that the improvement plan does not cover *all* activities on an inpatient unit. Specific improvement plans enable an inter-professional team to eliminate non-value-added activities, create flow and pull within the unit, reduce defects, and manage visually. The improvement will make the healthcare journey safer and more satisfying for patients. The completion of these plans will also move the key measures for the value stream while building internal capability in Lean improvement.

Let's review the kaizen activity for creating standard work to facilitate discharge planning and execution. Some patients stay in hospitals longer than necessary. This may, at least in part, be a result of the significant challenges faced by the unit at discharge time. To discharge a patient, the entire inter-professional team must participate and agree. To allow a patient to return home, staff must scramble to find the information, appointments, referrals, orders, and equipment needed for the discharge. After the discharge, another flurry of activity is required to assign the now-empty bed, clean it, prepare the next patient for transport and admission, and transfer the accountability of care. It is not surprising that some activities are overlooked, others are repeated, and mistakes are made—all of which represent waste that can be reduced or eliminated by implementing standard work for discharge planning.

When the improvement team at St. Xavier took a look at current conditions in the medical unit, they discovered that each member of the inter-professional team worked in his or her own "silo"—in an isolated way. While each discipline delivered its own set of tasks, there was no way of knowing which tasks were completed, which ones were late, and which ones were needed for today,

Table 4.14   Internal Medicine Improvement Plan

Activity	Impact
Standardize patient transfer to and from outside facilities	LOS, patient safety
Develop and implement joint inter-professional assessment	LOS, patient satisfaction
Create standard work for occupational therapy and physiotherapy	LOS, cost
Standardize nurse-to-nurse reporting	Patient safety, staff satisfaction
Implement standard work for wound protocols	LOS, patient safety
Implement standard work for pain management protocols	Patient satisfaction
Implement standard work for patient fall prevention	Patient safety, LOS
Update COPD and CHF evidence-based pathways	LOS
Create standard work for performing ADL	Patient satisfaction, cost, staff satisfaction
Create standard work for medicine administration	Patient safety
Create standard work for inter-professional discharge planning and execution	LOS
Improve turnaround time (from order to results) for diagnostic imaging	LOS
Improve turnaround time (from order to results) for laboratories	LOS
Implement 5S on unit	Staff satisfaction
Improve number of weekend discharges	LOS
Standardize teaching materials and patient education process	Patient satisfaction, reduce readmission rates

Table 4.14 *(Continued)*   Internal Medicine Improvement Plan

Develop process for daily inter-professional discharge promotion rounds	LOS
Implement medicine reconciliation	Patient satisfaction, accreditation standard

LOS = length of stay. COPD = chronic obstructive pulmonary disease. CHF = congestive heart failure. ADL = activities of daily living.

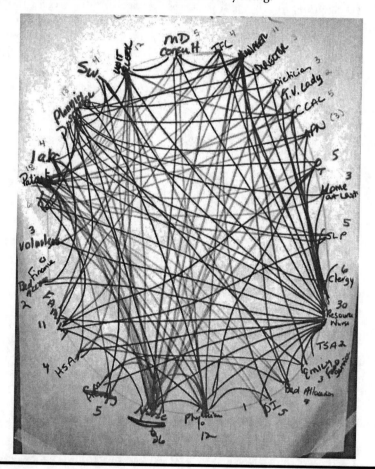

Figure 4.5   Current conditions of communication cycle.

tomorrow, etc. A Lean tool called the communication circle was used to show the hand-offs and communication waste in discharge planning. Figure 4.5 is an inpatient unit communication circle for discharge planning.

This circle reveals the hundreds of exchanges that occur as inter-professional members of the healthcare team communicate around discharge planning issues. Recall from Chapter 3 (Circle diagram section) that the different roles involved in the process are identified on the outside of the circle. For this case study, we have over 25 different roles that have a part in the treatment and discharge planning for the patient. These roles include the physician, the nurse, all of the members of the allied health team including physiotherapy, and speech language pathology, and the services that provide therapeutics and diagnostics including pharmacy, diagnostic imaging and laboratory services. In discharge planning, staff members frequently have no way of knowing the complete picture of a patient because bits and pieces of status information lie with different professionals and staff members. Because every person's understanding is specific to his or her discipline and not shared, no member of the team has a complete picture. This is why a common electronic medical record is needed. In this case, the organization already had a shared electronic documentation system.

Wastes and their sources were identified from the current process as shown in Table 4.15. The Lean concepts of flow, pull, and defect-free helped the team

Table 4.15 Key Wastes in Internal Medicine

Key Waste	Root Causes
Expected date of discharge (EDD) not known	No consistent way to communicate to family; EDD determined too late to properly prepare for timely discharge; EDD not consistently documented
Fragmented communication	Information not transparent; no known discharge criteria; no standard point of contact between staff and family
No clear patient goals established	Discharge plan not visual for staff, patient, family; patient boards not consistently updated; team rounds held only weekly
Patient education inconsistent and inadequate	Fears and anxieties not addressed consistently; activities of daily living education meets patient needs inconsistently; lack of formal process for patient education
Discharge delayed by late referrals	No clear triggers for referrals; rounds held weekly; confusion about how referrals are triggered
Excessive discharge workload on day of discharge	Standard discharge protocol not in place; no standard work established

eliminate these key wastes. Creating flow allowed staff to line up the steps in the correct sequence in a standardized way. Pull enabled staff to consistently trigger work in a timely manner. Defect-free led staff to eliminate missing activity. By addressing the root causes using a Lean approach, key wastes were resolved. However, visual management was likely the most important element in the improvement of discharge planning at this hospital. It was essential to create transparency in the process so that each team member could immediately see patient status and whether the conditions were normal or abnormal. Abnormal conditions require immediate attention, so they needed to be identified at a glance.

After creating the standard work for the different segments of discharge planning and creating common and consistent triggers to perform the work, the team created a discharge planning visual management system. This new system (Figure 4.6) allowed immediate visual assessment of the entire unit from one location. On a patient-by-patient basis, the discharge planning activity could be seen by the entire inter-professional team.

The top portion (first five lines) of the board provides the basic information about the patient such as the room number, physician, admission date, etc. This section also notes an expected date of discharge. The next section communicates the inter-professional discharge goals. When all the goals are met, the patient can be discharged. One of the key values of this system is that everyone can

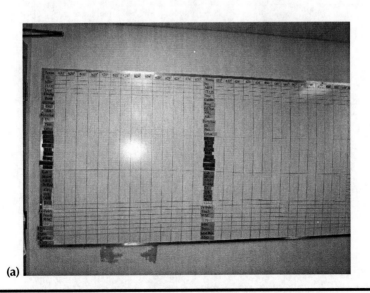

(a)

Figure 4.6 (a) Overview. Discharge planning visual management system. (b) Close-up. (From HHCC kaizen [5S in ED] and HHCC kaizen [medicine–discharge planning]. With permission.)

Room	620^1	620^2	620^3	620^4	622^1	62
Int.						
MRP						
TLOS						
Dest						
Cardio						
Resp						
GI/Nut.						
GU						
Act.						
Psyhc/Soc						
Dx.						
Pain						
Other						
PT						
RT						
Plan						
CCAC						
SLP						
Nutr.						
IPAC						
Nursing						
Other						
Lab						
Micro						
ARO						
X-Ray						
CT						
U/S						
OHB						
Tx						
EDD-2						
IV/Foley						
Teach						
IPAC						
EDD-1						
FPN						
Trans.						
Med Rec						
ADD						

Figure 4.6 (b)

see the same discharge goals at a glance. Moving down the board, the middle section lists the barriers to discharge, for example, waiting for a procedure, a consult, acceptance of an application, etc. Each barrier shows a due date for resolution. Late actions are addressed daily. The bottom section lists the standard work involved in the discharge; it details the actions that start two days before discharge: arranging transportation, ensuring that required home supports are in place, scheduling follow-up appointments, and making sure that medicine prescriptions are prepared and signed.

The discharge management system comes to life in daily discharge promotion rounds. During these rounds (which are distinct from regular medical rounds), every patient is reviewed every day by the complete inter-professional team including physicians. The focus is not on medical history and treatment plans reviewed during medical rounds. Discharge promotion rounds are concerned with factors that prevent patients from meeting their discharge goals. After the barriers are identified, actions to resolve them are assigned to the appropriate staff and physicians. Perhaps an intervention is needed to get a consult moving or action is required to expedite a procedure. Each patient has a plan and the plan is managed daily. The daily discharge promotion rounds covering all patients on a unit typically take about 10 or 15 minutes.

Upon discharge, the effectiveness of the discharge planning system is evaluated. The measurement is simple: did the patient meet the expected discharge date (EDD)? If the patient's length of stay exceeded the EDD, the cause of the exception (variance) is documented. The exceptions are then prioritized based on frequency so improvement can occur. Figure 4.7 shows a variance tracking system for tracking discharge planning effectiveness.

Before such charts were available, hospitals had no way to really understand why length-of-stay targets were achieved or missed without performing extensive chart audits. Tables like Figure 4.7 capture the information required to pinpoint the causes of longer-than-expected patient stays. To effectively use this Lean technique, we must capture the variance at the best time: the day the patient leaves. This way we know all of the causes of the variation and can capture them in just 10 seconds to deliver meaningful and accurate data that enables further improvement.

Within 18 months, all aspects of St. Xavier's value stream improvement plan were completed and at the end of the process, one final activity was added to the plan. Management saw an opportunity to consolidate roles. Redundancy was noted among the clinical coordinator, discharge planning, and resource utilization roles. The decision was made to create a "super role"—a new position in which one person would be responsible for all three functions, but using a smaller staff-to-patient ratio. The consolidation of roles combined with the lower ratio allowed the "super" staff member to provide superior customer service to a

Planned EDD	Actual D/C Date	Variance from Plan	Comments
10/20	10/21	+1	Couldn't arrange ride home
10/21	10/24	+3	No process to discharge on the weekend
10/21	10/21	0	Plan met
10/24	10/25	+1	Home supports arranged too late to make target date

Figure 4.7 Variance planning for discharge planning effectiveness.

Table 4.16 Summary of Results of Internal Medicine Value Stream

Measure	Baseline	Target	Actual	% Change
Access: reduce average length of stay	7.6 days	6.6 days	6.1 days	20% reduction
Quality: patients consistently treated using evidence-based care	32%	90%	94%	194% increase
Quality: readmission rate within 30 days of discharge	8.3%	3%	3.4%	59% decrease
Service quality: overall survey score	72%	85%	87%	21% increase

defined set of patients. When the standard work for this position was developed and implemented, the total full time equivalent requirement was five persons fewer, leading to redeployment of five nurses into the system! The results from the value stream improvement are summarized in Table 4.16.

Many people both within and outside of healthcare believe that patients do not spend enough time in hospitals. That is a debate we cannot solve in this book. What I can state is that everyone deserves the best, safest, timeliest care possible. Each patient also deserves to be discharged to his or her next location in a safe manner.

Using the tools, techniques, and applications of Lean, it is possible to safely reduce the lengths of stays on inpatient units while providing the best evidence-based care.

Beyond the Hospital: Continuing Care in the Community

Patients who leave an emergency room, clinic, or acute care setting often continue to require care—some of which extends beyond the hospital framework. This is particularly true of the aging population for whom physician visits, procedures, and examinations meet only a portion of their needs. In addition to professional healthcare treatment, this population also needs community support.

This type of support can mean anything from taking care of their homes (helping with snow shoveling or raking leaves, for example) or assisting with daily living (meal delivery or household help). For the particularly frail, community-based support may include personal assistance with taking a bath or organizing a daily medicine regimen. Chronic patients and those at the end of their lives may require support via pain management. If you have been a caregiver who tried to coordinate these services for a loved one, you know that this work can be time-consuming, snarled by applications and eligibility requirements, and just plain frustrating for the both caregiver and patient. The community supports available are often individual organizations that lack the ability to share information and services. The locations of the services and the boundaries of the areas served shift frequently. It's difficult to know whom to call. If English is your *second* language, your task is even more difficult. You must navigate the system (imperfect as it is) and surmount language and cultural barriers as well.

Our next case study demonstrates how a group of urban community agencies came together and made a difference for their clients using a Lean approach. The improvement took place in "Metropolis," a suburb of a large city of three million people. Metropolis was home to 600,000 people and has all the same conveniences and resources as the big city it adjoins. Residents raised complaints about the disjointedness of community programs to the city council for three years. They were frustrated with the programs until a city council person had to navigate a loved one through the system with significant difficulty. The issue was then brought to the regional health planning committee.

At the recommendation of the committee, over 20 community agencies, home nursing care, and acute hospital partners volunteered to collaborate to develop a new system with two clear objectives: (1) make it easier for seniors to access community services, and (2) connect community care partners to one another. The challenges were enormous. Some agencies had several thousand staff and others worked with a handful. Each agency had its own client files; some had electronic medical records, others ran entirely on paper systems.

Table 4.17 Kaizen Improvement Plan

Kaizen Event Topic
Develop common initial screening tool and intake assessment
Generate complete inventory of available services
Develop system for cultural and translation services
Develop senior transition and hand-off process from one agency to another
Develop standard work for call center operations

Table 4.18 Key Measures

Measure	Baseline	Target
Service quality: increased customer satisfaction	64%	80%
Staff morale: improved staff confidence in quality of information	38%	90%
Process quality: first time referrals made correctly	82%	95%
Access: reduced lead time for services	4 to 14 days	2 days

While the challenges were more complex than those in our other case studies and the improvement team was more varied and widespread, the effort started from the tried-and-true Lean starting point: value stream analysis. In this case, two current states instead of one had to be mapped. First, the team needed to understand how seniors accessed community services while they were in the hospital. Second, an analysis was required to determine how one community service accessed a different community service when a client showed a need: how community services talked to each other. After the value-stream analysis was completed, the resulting action plan yielded a series of quick wins, projects, and kaizen workshops. Table 4.17 is a partial summary of the kaizen activity. The improvement activities were custom designed to deliver improvement on the key measures cited in Table 4.18

Every client begins at the same place: he or she is screened to determine needs. The team decided to begin with the creation of a single standard intake tool to be used by all partners for screening clients. The activity began with an evaluation of the various intake forms in current use by the different partners. Figure 4.8 demonstrates the quantity and variety of intake forms in place when Lean improvement began.

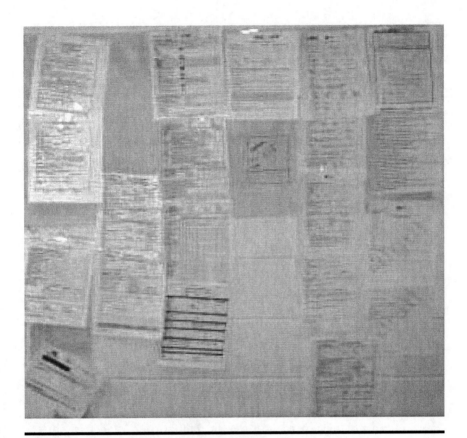

Figure 4.8   Intake forms—current condition.

Before the team could consolidate the forms, they had to identify the value added by the intake process by determining why initial screening was required. The team found two clear reasons for initial screening: (1) to gather demographic information about clients who needed services, and (2) to assess client needs. After value added was determined, the team identified common elements required in every intake screen:

1. Contact information for client (and caller if applicable)
2. Consent to share information
3. Language translation needs
4. Demographics to determine eligibility for services
5. Brief functional assessment to determine type of help needed
6. Client's willingness and/or ability to pay fees for some services
7. Client goals

The outputs of screening would be referrals to appropriate agencies. As a result of improvement, a new screening tool was completed and a script (what was to be said during screening) was devised to ensure consistency in the screening process and receiving consistent answers no matter who performed the screen. If the correct information was captured from clients via this improved process, the quality of referrals to servicing agencies would be much higher. (Remember, the quality of referral was a key measure for the value stream.) The time required to complete a screening increased slightly, compared to the time required for the previous process, but the quality of the information far outweighed the increase in time by eliminating downstream rework and clarification of information.

As the balance of the kaizen work was completed, several other standards were established. Before the improvement activity started, one agency had a contract to provide language translation services. Making this service available to all healthcare service providers in the network proved to be immediately beneficial. When providers found themselves in conversations with a client who could not speak English, they could now put the caller on hold, dial an 800 number, and add a translator to the conversation. The translation service offered virtually instantaneous access to over 200 languages and dialects, improving communication across the entire network of services and delighting the clients.

Another challenge was posed by geography: the areas serviced (and not serviced) by specific partners. Prior to improvement, phone calls had to be made to the various community partners to determine whether they serviced specific addresses. To eliminate the waste from the phone calls, maps were created to show the coverage areas of all providers. The maps were based on services. If you wanted meals delivered to a specific address, you could refer to the Meals-on-Wheels map to determine partner agencies' coverage areas. The maps were then converted to electronic files and hosted on a website for quick access.

Standards were implemented to ensure live hand-offs of all callers. Each screening agency was to ensure that a caller was connected in real time to the correct partner agency that could meet his or her needs. Before improvement was made, the agency receiving the referral would contact the client later—causing undue waiting and anxiety for the client. In the improved system, any caller receiving a referral for service would be put on hold and connected directly with the new servicing agency. This was a great benefit for every caller, in a world where many phone calls are impersonal and answered electronically, involving many difficult-to-navigate prompts and holds. The live hand-off was a significant improvement.

In this complex study of multi-agency improvement, the last big hurdle was determining who in which agency would answer the phone and handle screening. No single agency had a large enough call center or enough staff, to handle all the incoming calls. To solve this problem, a final kaizen event was held. It was a process preparation kaizen, called a 2P event by Lean practitioners. The purpose of the event was to determine how to perform the intake screening and assessment for the system without creating a new call center.

As with all kaizen events, a small team was identified to pursue improvement. An assortment of 12 people with skills including call center operations, phone and Internet expertise, and facilities design assembled for four days to design the new process for answering the phones and performing intake screening and assessment. A 2P kaizen event uses creativity to develop a new process. The improvement activity begins by determining the voice of the customer. Small focus groups are used to determine the needs of the customer, staff, and the organization (or in this case, organizations). These needs are translated into key criteria that must be met by a new design. In the kaizen event for this case study, the team identified the following key criteria:

1. Address culture and language sensitivity
2. Deliver first-time call resolution
3. Provide support throughout service access process
4. Enable easy access into system
5. No waiting
6. Defect- and redundancy-free operation
7. Fiscal responsibility
8. Point of use access to tools

After the key criteria were determined, the core processes of the call center were identified. The basic tasks were to:

1. Answer telephone calls
2. Provide language interpretation
3. Gather demographic information
4. Identify client needs and develop service plan
5. Transfer captured information to receiving partner
6. Document information
7. Acknowledge entry of client into system

Conducting a process preparation kaizen involves devising different solutions for each core process—many ways to accomplish the same required goal. Typically, seven solutions are identified, each providing a different way to deliver the core process. Let's look at Core Process 2 (provide language interpretation). These alternate methods were identified for the core process:

1. Use in-house staff and transfer call
2. Use external language service
3. Utilize computer software

4. Transfer call to an ethno-specific service provider that works in that language
5. Utilize a family member to translate
6. Use telephone software to route calls based on language selection decision trees
7. Utilize volunteers to assist in translation

After the seven potential solutions were identified, they were evaluated against the key criteria. In a 2P kaizen, evaluation is carried out via a Pugh analysis—a mathematical matrix for evaluating multiple criteria against multiple alternatives. The analysis uses a simple scoring technique. If a solution supports the criteria, it receives a score of 1. If the solution is at odds with the evaluation criteria, it scores –1. If the solution has no impact on the criteria, it is scored as 0. Scores are then added. The potential solution with the highest score is likely to best meet the key criteria. Our goal at this point in the kaizen is to generate several solutions that best meet all of key criteria. You can see how the analysis played out in Table 4.19.

The alternatives that scored the highest were external language services and family members (5 and 6). Pugh analyses were completed for all the other core processes as well. As each core process was analyzed, the solutions with the three highest scores advanced to the next round where they could be combined with other solutions to build an entire system.

After the call center system was designed to best meet the key criteria, the team completed the standard work to operate the call center. After that, a capital plan and an operational plan were created and one-time, start-up expenses were identified. (All of this was completed in four days!)

After about 12 weeks, the capital plan was approved and implemented and the call center became operational. Perhaps the most impressive aspect of the call center story is that no additional personnel resources were required to accomplish the improvement, Existing technology was used to link the partner agencies. Using an interconnected phone system, calls went to the four largest agencies first. If a call was not answered by the fourth ring, the phones in all the remaining agencies rang simultaneously. The common screen and intake assessment ensured consistency regardless of which agency answered the call. The interconnected phone system also allowed easy transfer of clients to receiving agencies; a call was never terminated until it was successfully connected to a partner agency and next steps were clear for all parties.

After the entire value stream improvement plan was completed, a comprehensive training package was developed and delivered to the individual agencies. The results from the value stream improvement are highlighted in Table 4.20. Despite the complexities presented by multiple service partners and a broad geographical area, this team of healthcare professionals was able to make significant improvements in service quality by using Lean.

Table 4.19 Pugh Analysis for Providing Translation Services

	Culture and Language Sensitivity	First-Call Resolution	Constant Support	Easy Access into System	No Waiting	Freedom from Defects and Redundancy	Fiscal Responsibility	Point of Use Tools	Pugh Score
In-house staff	1	1	1	1	-1	0	0	0	3
External language service	1	1	1	1	1	1	-1	0	5
Computer software	1	1	-1	-1	1	0	-1	0	0
Ethno-specific agency	1	1	1	0	-1	1	0	0	3
Family members	1	0	1	1	1	1	1	0	6
Telephone software routing	1	1	-1	-1	0	0	-1	0	-1
Volunteers	1	1	1	1	-1	0	1	0	4

Table 4.20 Summary of Value Stream Improvement

Measure	Baseline	Target	Actual	% Change
Service quality: increased consumer satisfaction	64%	80%	82%	28% increase
Staff morale: improved staff confidence in quality of information	38%	90%	94%	147% increase
Process quality: first time referrals made correctly	82%	95%	98%	19.5% increase
Access: reduced lead time for services	4 to 14 days (average 6.8 days)	2 days	3.7 days (average)	46% decrease

Creating More Time for Quality Care: Streamlining Administration

Our healthcare system is continually challenged to find better ways to deliver value. Meanwhile, our ability to deliver value to patients is constantly impacted by administrative requirements, insurance and billing requirements, and needs for management data. While we can agree that these activities add some value to our organizations, a significant amount of activity adds *no* value for patients and acts as a source of frustration for staff and medical professionals who are burdened with data collection and entry. Electronic systems certainly help with information sharing and are essential for aggregating and disaggregating data in charts and management tools. Still, someone must physically enter data into the system and that's a core problem. For many people, data entry is more time-consuming than completing a paper form. Every time consuming data-entry task represents time that could be spent with patients.

Our final case study looks at patient registration—a core function of every healthcare organization. Patient registration has engendered many debates in healthcare. Should registration be centralized or decentralized? Should the process also include order entry or only core registration data entry (demographics and insurance information)? How can registration aid patient safety? Should registration collect clinical data? As you can see, what appears a relatively straightforward clerical function involves many issues that are difficult to resolve.

Table 4.21   Kaizen Measures and Targets for Patient Registration

Dimension	Measure	Baseline	Target
Service	Patient satisfaction: survey scores on specific questions related to registration	62%	90%
Quality and financial	Information quality: uncollectible billings due to wrong information	$9450/month	Reduce 75% to $2363/month
Productivity	Time per registration	5 minutes	Reduce 25% to 3.75 minutes

In our final case study, the improvement team at the fictional Metropolitan Medical Center examined the activities comprising standard work for patient registration. Improvement came about as a result of a kaizen event. The kaizen preparation began by defining the measures and targets shown in Table 4.21. The team started by defining the current conditions. The kaizen activity began with the creation of a flow map of the work. Because registration occurred at more than 50 locations within the organization, a number of different workflows were documented. After they were identified and mapped, the team completed time observations on the registration process by measuring the cycle times in four departments. The time to complete a registration ranged from less than 1 minute to more than 7 minutes.

The team reassembled and documented the wastes of the current registration process. A few of the key wastes and their direct causes are summarized in Table 4.22. The data quality in the current process delivered a 0% yield: not a *single* registration was completed properly with all the appropriate fields filled out. Entire sections of the registration system were missed and patient identification was not checked or verified consistently. Of course, the process varied from person to person—different registration clerks missed different parts of the process.

After the root causes of the wastes were determined, the team moved to establish solutions for them. Like all the previous improvements we discussed, the principles of flow, pull, zero defects, visual management, and continuous improvement guided the thinking. The core improvement principle used for this event was standard work.

The team reviewed each field in the registration screen and traced the field back to the requesting source. When this activity was completed, the team identified seven pieces of captured information that were not needed by other parts of the organization. These items were immediately eliminated. For the remaining

Table 4.22   Registration Wastes and Root Causes

Waste	Root Causes
Overproduction of patient wrist bands	Not standardized within organization; allergy bands not computer generated
Variability in registration process	No clear standards for required fields
Rework caused by late patient arrival	Parking problem; lack of standard guidelines for arrival time; poor signage and unclear path
Poor data quality	No standard for fields; free text utilized; no accountability for data quality
Time lost scrolling through screens	Standard product requires data entry on seven screens
Patient delays due to late registration	Registration staff handles non-registration duties; registration not dedicated job function; work not standardized; no accountability in current process

fields, data entry standards were created so that each field would contain consistent information. In many cases, pull-down boxes with predetermined choices were used to eliminate "free text" (a blank field to be filled in) and standardize the selection of answers. Because information in the remaining fields was needed by other parts of the organization, the completion of all fields was required; no sections could be skipped. To standardize the collection of registration data, scripts were created so that the registration clerks would ask the patients for the necessary information. Because some questions dealt with sensitive subjects such as financial information and religious affiliation, the scripts were a great help for the clerks.

To eliminate time wasted by scrolling through screens, the sequence was rearranged to allow a more logical flow. This saved time needed to move from one screen to the next and back. The change in screen flow and question flow eliminated two screens from the registration process and shortened data entry time. Other solutions for the key wastes are listed in Table 4.23.

The results of the kaizen event met expectations. Testing of the new process was completed on the third day and standard work that incorporated all the changes was developed and documented. Training plans were developed and the new process was rolled out on a department-by-department basis over the next 60 days. Table 4.24 summarizes the kaizen improvement.

During the event, the takt time was calculated for the registration process. Takt time was a "moving target" because different departments had different

Table 4.23 Solutions to Key Wastes

Waste	Root Causes	Solutions
Overproduction of wrist bands	Not standardized within organization; allergy bands not computer generated	Standards created for use and color of armbands
Variability in registration process	No clear standards for required fields	Standard created for each field; pull-down boxes added to eliminate free text
Rework caused by late patient arrival	Parking problems; no standard guidelines for arrival time; poor signage and path directions	Standard arrival times; improved directions and signs
Poor data quality	No standards for fields; free text utilized; no accountability for data quality	Standard created for each field; pull-down boxes added to eliminate free text; developed data quality audit
Time lost scrolling through screens	Standard product requires data entry into seven screens	Changed screen and field flow; eliminated unneeded data
Patient delays due to late registration	Registration staff handles nonregistration duties; registration not dedicated job function; work not standardized; no accountability in current process	Created standard work; built accountability systems with visual management

hours of operation and patient volumes. The takt time had to be calculated for each hour and on a department-by-department basis. When the cycle times were finalized and the process improved from 5 to 4.1 minutes per registration, the minimum staffing calculation was determined.

The net result of the cycle time reduction over the course of a day was the equivalent of 5.5 full-time registration clerks. As a result, three staff associates changed their work hours to provide more coverage on nights and weekends, taking the registration burden off clinical staff and resulting in more time for patient care! The other 2.5 staff members were redeployed to other open positions in the hospital, resulting in a financial savings. As a result of the

Table 4.24 Kaizen Improvement Summary

Dimension	Measure	Baseline	Target	Actual	Change %
Service	Patient satisfaction: survey scores on specific questions about registration	62%	90%	88%	42% increase
Quality and financial	Information quality: uncollectible billings due to wrong information	$9450/month	Reduce 75% to $2363/ month	$1380/month	85% reduction
Productivity	Time per registration	5 minutes	Reduce 25% to 3.75 minutes	4.1 minutes	18% reduction
Quality	Data integrity	0% yield	100% yield	96%	N/A

improvement in collections brought about by solving the data integrity issues and the redeployment of associates, the net fiscal savings to the corporation exceeded $250,000 per year. Just look at the returns from a 4-day kaizen event: huge savings, increased patient satisfaction, and clinical staff made available for more value-added work. Pretty impressive!

Summary

Each of these case studies is unique. And each of them probably reflects some aspect of your healthcare organization. Across North America, hospitals, clinics, and community care agencies face common challenges that impact their ability to provide consistent, accessible, high quality care. One of the beauties of Lean improvement is its flexibility. Its methods can be applied in any workplace and customized to address specific challenges. Many organizations are surprised when they discover how much improvement can be made in a short time, such as the 4-day kaizen event described above. This immediate pay-off is not unusual at all when Lean thinking is applied. What case study are you facing? Imagine the rewards ahead for your organization—and the benefits that will be passed along to your patients—when you put Lean thinking into practice.

Chapter 5

Getting Started

To this point we have covered why improvement is imperative in healthcare. We also discussed the fundamentals of improvement and several of the common tools used to see and eliminate waste. We then reviewed the application of these tools through case studies, showing what is possible when teams are empowered to act on a targeted opportunity. I hope you are intrigued by the possibility of what the application of Lean can do for your organization.

The next question that usually arises is, "How do we get started?" If you have no idea where to begin, getting started can be difficult. In my experience, however, most organizations have at least a general idea where their opportunities lie. As a result, simply taking the first step is the most important action. Here's how to start. Pick a highly visible area in your organization and begin by mapping the value stream. Remember, a value stream consists of all the activities that deliver value to your customers.

In a healthcare setting, it's very rare for the improvement process to begin in a non-clinical area. This fact does not diminish the value of a hospital's administrative processes; however, it reflects the fact that in healthcare the value-added areas are assessment, diagnosis, treatment, education, and discharge of patients. (If you're thinking that prevention is another important element in today's model for healthcare, I agree. Additional value-added activities are those that prevent the need for hospital care.) Regardless of where you begin, I'd like to offer you a roadmap that will enhance your chances of success:

1. Define your measurable outcomes.
2. Select and map your value streams.
3. Begin improvement.

4. Sustain your improvement and manage visually.
5. Support your improvement with training and coaching.
6. Spread your improvements.

Following these six steps in order will assist you to create a culture of improvement. Let's cover the steps in more detail.

Define Measurable Outcomes

Improvement begins by combining clear measures of success with an agreed-upon definition of how success will be measured. World class organizations use "true north" measures to drive improvement. Measures of operational excellence can be grouped according to a few indicators. These indicators are used in Lean organizations to show the direction in which the organization is heading. The compass analogy and the "true north" term derive from the concept of direction. Ideally, an entire organization will be aligned and focused on these targets. Excellence is created by simultaneously improving the five improvement dimensions shown in Table 5.1.

In the context of getting started in improvement, we first want to define the outcome measures for the entire organization. We can define these as "board-level" outcome measures that create the focus for the organization. Table 5.2 lists examples of key corporate outcome measures for a hospital system.

In strategy discussions, we frequently hear references to a "balanced scorecard" for addressing multiple dimensions of an organization's overall activity. For example, a hospital must balance overall productivity with evidence-based

Table 5.1 True North Measures

Dimension	True North Measure
Morale and staff development	Staff morale or staff engagement measures
Quality	Clinical outcomes, patient safety measures, and measures of process quality
Delivery and access	Lead times for goods and services from "customer need identified" to "customer need met" expressed in minutes, hours, or days
Cost	Resource hours or dollars consumed per unit of service
Growth	Increases in volumes or revenues

Table 5.2 Key Corporate Outcome Measures

Dimension	Corporate Outcome Measure
Morale/People Development	Increase the percentage of staff participating on an improvement team in the first year by 30%
Quality	Reduce preventable mortality and morbidity by 85%
Access	Reduce the wait time for hospital services by 50%
Cost/Productivity	Reduce the corporate labor hours per patient bed day by 15%
Growth	Expand clinic visit volume levels by 10%

practice, patient safety, community access, and other dimensions. The intent is to not increase risk to the organization, for example, by shortchanging evidence-based practice in favor of improving productivity. If we improved productivity without taking evidence-based practice into account, we would risk compromising patient safety outcomes. The balanced scorecard approach minimizes risks to patients and the organization.

Here's another example. We could expand the number of clinic visits by adding staff. However, without a balancing measure of productivity or cost, we would improve the visit measurement—at the expense of overall cost. This kind of well-meaning but shortsighted decision-making occurs frequently. Management decisions are often driven by measurement and evaluation—two powerful motivators for managers at every level. However, as we apply Lean thinking, we are trying to create a culture of improvement where waste is continuously eliminated from processes. The *only* way to simultaneously improve morale, quality, access, and cost and growth measures is to eliminate non-value-added (NVA) activities. By using the true north measures that cover all five dimensions of operational excellence, you can generate the correct behaviors from management that will lead to genuine improvement.

Select and Map Value Streams

Now that we have defined the organization's outcome measures, the next step is to identify and map the key value streams within the organization. With the outcomes now determined, we can perform analysis to find the areas to direct our improvement efforts. For example, if we want to improve patient satisfaction, we should go to an area of the organization where the patient satisfaction scores are low. Patient satisfaction falls under the true north dimension of service quality. If we want to increase access to services, we should focus on the areas with the

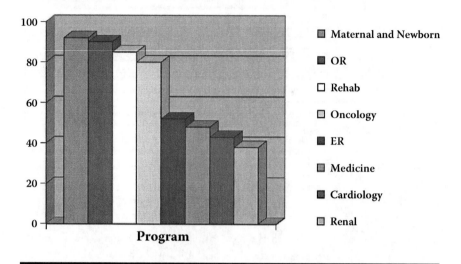

Figure 5.1   Pareto analysis of staff satisfaction by program.

longest wait times. One way to analyze your organization is to use a histogram (more commonly called a Pareto diagram) with data prioritized from highest to lowest to help make sense of your comparison data. Figure 5.1 is a Pareto diagram for sorting administrative staff and medical staff satisfaction by program.

As you review this data, keep a few points in mind. First, remember that a value stream includes all activities, both good and bad, involved in delivering value to customers. A value stream is *not* a department, program, or unit. Analyzing data by individual programs makes sense because it is easy to understand geography, resource requirements, and budgets. In application, when we map a value stream, we see that the customer experience actually crosses several departments. For example, a single visit to an emergency department can impact the emergency staff, patient registration, laboratory, pharmacy, diagnostic imaging, and environmental services.

Second, as we return to our discussion of selecting and mapping the key value streams, we ask how this data can be interpreted. In terms of improvement potential, clearly the leverage lies within the four areas circled in Figure 5.2. After you select key value streams, you will want to organize your cross-functional team and map the streams. We reviewed the concept of value stream mapping in Chapter 3. Remember that the key outputs of a value stream analysis are the measures and targets that create a focus for improvement and drive the right organizational behavior and detailed improvement plan. Current state and future state mappings are valuable tools to help us see and eliminate waste but are secondary in importance to the key measures and improvement plan.

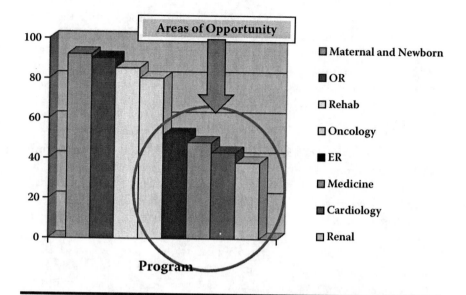

Figure 5.2   Areas of leverage for improving satisfaction scores.

When determining the key measures for the value stream, it's important to understand one important concept. After the organizational outcome measures are defined, the next step is to define the value stream outcome measures. Each value stream engaged will have measures that must align with the organization's measures. If we fail to align the measures, then the great improvement work in preparing the value stream will not tie back to the outcome measures for the organization. I have seen this happen more than once and assure you that this lack of alignment can have devastating effects on your continuous improvement journey.

For example, assume we have a corporate goal to improve access to services by 30%. This goal must be deployed to the value stream level. Assume further that perioperative service (surgery) is the value stream we wish to improve to impact the corporate measure. We now need a value stream measure specific to peri-operative services that aligns with the corporate target. An example of an aligning value stream measure would be to increase volumes through the surgical clinic by 50%. Why not select a 30% target, after all that is the corporate target? I find it best to stretch the value stream measure to ensure we hit the corporate target.

Sooner or later (and usually sooner) someone will ask why the Lean efforts are not moving the "big dot" (true north) measures on the corporate scorecard. The reasons can be twofold. First, the outcome measures may not be aligned; as a result, improvement work at the tactical level may not constitute improvement at the strategic level. Second, the collection of the organization's tactical improvement may not be enough to move an entire corporate measure. For example, even if you make a heroic effort to improve patient satisfaction scores in food services, you may not impact enough patients to move the corporate patient satisfaction measure. We may only realize the desired corporate improvement when patient satisfaction scores in food services, general surgery, day surgery, and pharmacy services all improve at the same time. We need to improve in enough areas to move the big dots.

We can live with that scenario when improvement efforts are just beginning. We know that we can always add value streams and eventually improve broadly across the organization while also achieving improvement more quickly. However, there is no fix for unaligned measures. Improving faster, broader, or deeper will *never* resolve the disconnect between organizational and strategic measures, so it is imperative that we create the alignment *before* we begin improving.

Many organizations want to jump right into improvement, but I do not encourage that approach. If you begin improvement too early, you are likely to start working on the wrong things. I define a "wrong" approach as an improvement that is not strategic (does not align with the corporate true north measures), or activity that fails to deliver value to customers. When the first steps taken are nonstrategic or non-value-added, many organizations stop their improvement activities because they see them (incorrectly) as expenses without returns. That's why it is essential to start improvement by using the right measures to work on the right targets. You will not want to take shortcuts in the first few steps. The appropriate start will help you achieve the expected results.

Begin Improvement

What have we accomplished thus far? Your organization has agreed on the true north outcome measures using a balanced scorecard approach and selected the appropriate value streams to help move the outcome measures. You have performed a value stream analysis on critical issues and now have value stream measures that align with the outcome measures and a detailed improvement plan to improve your value stream. Having completed all this work, you have now earned the right to improve.

We already covered several tools used to see and eliminate waste. We also reviewed the improvement approaches commonly used in Lean improvement: the kaizen event, A3, and 5S (Chapter 3). Now I offer a few suggestions for optimizing your improvement launch.

As we discussed earlier in this chapter, follow your value stream plans. It will be tempting to jump into a kaizen event or A3 on some painful area and skip the steps of focusing on a few key value streams, aligning the measures to the corporate scorecard, completing the value stream, and developing a plan to deliver your future state vision. Remember, rarely does improving a spot area add up to meaningful change for the organization or its customers. Stay focused on your original plan.

Use a consistent approach as you improve. Several improvement approaches in addition to Lean are commonly used today. You may be familiar with Six Sigma, Business Process Reengineering, the Theory of Constraints, Project Management, and the Plan–Do–Check–Act approaches. It takes a lifetime to master any one of them and they all present very steep learning curves. I often see organizations use different improvement approaches in different departments. This is typically the result of a lack of clear organizational strategy for improvement and each department chooses what it believes is its best course for getting results. When an organization uses more than one improvement approach, a great deal of confusion can be experienced by the leadership, staff, and medical team. In time, you may choose to introduce a wider menu of improvement approaches, but at the beginning I encourage you to pick just one. This book is about Lean and that is my bias. But regardless of the approach you choose, you will make your learning curve easier and maximize your results if you begin with a single consistent approach.

It is helpful to build some organizational discipline before starting on standard work. The foundation for discipline is 5S. Recall that 5S is a management system for creating a high performing work area. This system organizes material, supplies, equipment, and information in a manner that promotes standard work while making work areas safer and cleaner. Beginning your improvement with 5S is recommended for four reasons. It (1) promotes a good work environment, (2) creates improved administrative staff and medical staff satisfaction, (3) builds discipline in the staff, and (4) is designed to be managed visually. All the habits needed to manage process control can be learned by managing a 5S system.

Involve the right team to do the work. Some simple tools can help identify the right team members to design and implement the improvements. The team members we need must be relevant to the process we are studying. The definition of a process is a series of activities that convert inputs to outputs. A very simple way to define a process is to use an IPO (inputs, process, and outputs) diagram such as the example in Figure 5.3.

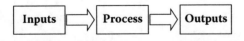

Figure 5.3   Input, process, and output (IPO) diagram.

As an example, let's say you visit the clinic of your primary care physician because you have a sinus infection. The trigger for this process is the infection that created your need to see a physician. The process is completed when you leave the clinic with a diagnosis and a prescription for antibiotics. The process inputs are:

- Patient condition
- Insurance information
- Prior medical history
- Current medicine profile

The high level clinic visit process steps are:

- Schedule visit
- Check in and register at office
- Visit with medical assistant
- Visit with physician
- Check out

The outputs of the process are:

- Diagnosis
- Updated medical history
- Prescription
- Data (visit time, appointment or billing code, dictated visit notes, etc.)

Figure 5.4 is an IPO diagram for a clinic visit.

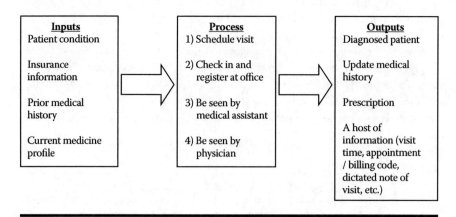

Figure 5.4   Input, process, and output (IPO) diagram for clinic visit.

Now that we have completed the IPO diagram, we can identify the right team members to be involved in improvement. The team should include representation from the functions that supply the inputs, perform the process, and receive the outputs. The suppliers of the inputs are the patient and perhaps the health records personnel. The people whose work is part of the process include the registration clerk, medical assistant, and physician. The customers of the outputs are the patient, health records team, pharmacy staff, and management. Based on these IPO factors, the team needed to work to improve clinic processes must include:

- A patient
- Health records associate
- Registration clerk
- Medical assistant
- Physician
- Pharmacy employee
- Administrative manager

What would happen if we omitted one of these key stakeholders? One possibility is moving the waste around the system. For example, we make the coding and billing processes more difficult by eliminating information needed by that department. The intent was to expedite documentation by the clinic staff. Even if this is an unintended consequence of the improvement, we have taken waste from one operation (the clinic) and moved it to another (health records). This is not an improvement. Waste must be eliminated—leave the system. Keep in mind that simply shifting waste from one department to another is not an improvement.

If we omit the clinic process from the improvement activity, we fail to create buy-in to change. Without staff buy-in, you will find yourself trying to change staff members instead of allowing them to initiate ideas that will change their performance and the system. To initiate improvement, you can involve the people who do the work in generating solutions or offer your own solutions. Which approach do you think has a higher degree of success?

Pick the right targets. When you begin improvement, you must monitor two sets of measures: the outcome measures (aligned to both the value stream and the corporate scorecard) and the process measures. During day-to-day operations, you must pay attention to the process to deliver the appropriate outcome.

Let me expand on this concept with a simple example. When a patient arrives on an inpatient unit, he or she wants to achieve an outcome: wellness. At the end of the inpatient visit, he or she has achieved a certain state of wellness that allows safe discharge. During the visit, however, we do not pay attention to the outcome. Instead, we use process measures to see whether the patient is on a trajectory to wellness. The process measures we focus on may be vital signs (trending favorably), oxygen saturation, and laboratory markers. If the vital signs, oxygen saturation, and lab values trend favorably throughout the visit, we know that the patient is moving toward wellness. Likewise, in improvement we must pay attention to both process and results.

Let's look at another example: trying to reduce the number of pressure ulcers in the intensive care unit. The first step is to calculate the outcome measure. At the end of the month, we find a total of one affected patient. Pressure ulcer incidence is usually calculated as a ratio dividing the number of pressure ulcers by the number of patient bed days. In this example, the number of bed days per month is 20 beds × 30 days = 600; the pressure ulcer rate is 1 ÷ 600 or .00167 ulcers per bed day. This ratio is the outcome measure. Next, we determine process measure. According to current evidence-based best practice, we should turn eligible patients every 2 hours to prevent pressure ulcers. We can analyze our adherence to this best practice as a way to determine our process measure.

If we set a target of 100% compliance to the best practice, our process measure will therefore be the percentage of patients that are appropriately turned every 2 hours. Determining the percentage requires a daily audit of the system. Using the process measure as our guide, we arrive at a hypothesis: as the process measure rate increases (as a result of adherence to best practice), the pressure ulcer rate should decrease. I will caution you that it takes time to develop the skills for generating great outcome and process measures. Generally speaking, improvement teams find it easier to determine outcome measures. (Remember to make sure the outcome aligns with the strategy!)

Process measures are more difficult to capture because they usually require real-time data capture. Unfortunately many of the process measures of healthcare are not automated and data must be captured manually. Don't forget to use the process control board—one of the most effective tools to eliminate waste. The board is designed to monitor process and can therefore be very valuable for process measure analysis.

Start yesterday. My last helpful hint in beginning improvement is start immediately. If we follow the model for improvement, we first select our outcome measures, then select and map value streams to create clear, prioritized improvement plans. These initial steps will create strong momentum for change arising from a value stream: the staff will be energized to begin. If improvement is delayed, you will lose valuable momentum.

When is the best time plant a tree? The answer: 25 years ago! The same is true for Lean improvement. As a leader in your organization (whether your leadership role is formal or informal), you want a motivated and inspired staff, great quality outcomes for your patients, reduced lead times to enable better access, lower overall costs, and increased patient volumes. We have discussed how a Lean system—one that continuously sees and eliminates waste—can deliver double-digit improvements of performance and culture. What are you waiting for?

Sustain Improvement and Manage Visually

Now that you have begun your improvement, the "real" work begins. In following our model for improvement, we identified the key outcomes and value streams that provide the leverage, mapped the value streams to create our vision for creating flow and pull to eliminate waste, developed detailed action plans to create the future state, and began improvement to realize the future state. All this work will be in vain if we fail to build systems that sustain these improvements. Without question, the most difficult part of implementing a culture of continuous improvement is to sustain the improvements realized from the efforts of your improvement teams.

What exactly do we mean by "sustain"? Sustaining is carrying out all the activities needed to keep waste out of our new processes. In Lean healthcare, the management work is significantly different from what we currently do (remember the earlier discussion about unlearning what we know). If your improvement team followed the Lean approaches for identifying waste and used the improvement concepts of flow, pull, and defect-free to create and implement a new process, we *know* that waste has been removed from the system. Now that we have these new conditions, management must work equally hard (or harder) to keep the waste out of the system. The work required to sustain (keep waste out) is often called Lean management.

Lean management is a system of tools and activities that create the focus and staff engagement that will both keep the waste out and also remove even more waste from the system. When done well, Lean management enables you to actually create the conditions to do better *every* day!

The key tool in Lean management systems is visual management. As we learned in Chapter 2, visual management creates conditions that allow you to distinguish normal from abnormal at a glance, so actions can be taken in real time to maintain high quality, promote good flow, and maintain standard work. As we start our improvement, we must become adept at using three integral Lean tools of visual management: 5S, process control, and results management to sustain our improvement. It is essential for anyone new to Lean improvement to spend whatever time is necessary to get comfortable with the tools and techniques of visual management and ensure that management at all levels in the organization competently use them. Let's briefly cover the three topics.

5S

As we discussed earlier, 5S is an integral part of visual management and sustaining since it creates the conditions and culture to enable a high performing work area. Organizing the workplace in a way that fosters superior quality, promotes standard work flows, and eliminates the waste of hunting and searching is key to creating a Lean culture. Additionally, since a 5S workplace is managed in a way that allows everyone to differentiate normal from abnormal conditions, the spirit of visual management is met. Keeping the workplace organized and self improving are sustaining activities that help keep waste out of a system.

Here's another important note. Many organizations fail to sustain because management does not hold staff accountable for their actions. For example, not following proper standard work is likely to produce poor quality outcomes and increased cost. A robust 5S system will build discipline and address accountability issues in any operation.

Process Control

We covered the process control tool in Chapter 3. This tool shows how a process performs against the takt time of the operation. By now, we have a process control board posted. The hourly units are documented on the board and when the plan is not met, the sources of variation are documented on a frequency chart. Figure 5.5 shows a process control system consisting of a process control board for CT scanning and a frequency chart showing sources of variation from plan.

Now that we have data on the sources of variation, we can use problem solving to eliminate additional sources of waste. The process control board and frequency chart for CT scanning in the figure indicate that the leading sources of variation are unsigned requisitions. How will we resolve this issue? Who is responsible and when will the problem be resolved? The sustaining activities and the Lean management system consist of management activities that (1) ensure the process control board data is complete and accurate, (2) reveal the most significant sources of variation from plan, (3) ensure that corrective actions are in place, and (4) communicate status to all affected staff. Let's look at each management activity.

The only way to ensure that the process control data is complete and accurate is to audit its use. I recommend an hourly audit, but you may need to build up to that frequency. This requirement may appear daunting but hourly audits are already norms in industry and have been for 20 years! Management standard work is developed to allocate time to managers to review the visual management systems. As you get started, you will want to pay close attention to the 5S and process control systems. Figure 5.6 shows management standard work for a hospital charge nurse over a 12-hour shift.

Process Control Board for CT Scanning

Hour	Plan	Actual	Comments
0700-0800	4	3	Requisition not signed
0801-0900	4	4	
0901-1000	4	4	
1001-1100	4	3	Left vs. right body part not noted
1101-1200	4	4	
1201-1300	4	3	Outpatient failed to show
1301-1400	4	4	
1401-1500	4	4	

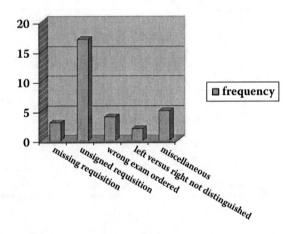

Figure 5.5 Process control and frequency charts.

Note that establishing the standard work for this nursing position accomplished a couple of key objectives. First, we budgeted time that allows the charge nurse to pay attention to the process control system. In addition to reviewing results, he or she can also improve the system by assigning tasks to the staff. Second, we cascaded the standard work by creating overlap with the manager from 1501 to 1600. This provides time for the manager to mentor the charge nurse and allows the charge nurse to escalate any issues outside her scope to the manager. In addition, the charge nurse and the manager can review the status of current action items to reduce sources of variation identified in the process control system. Management standard work ensures the dedication of time and

Time	Activity
0700–0800	Take report, review staffing and ensure coverage, audit night 5S results
0801–0900	Review visuals, assign one task for improvement, record any abnormal conditions on frequency chart
0901–1000	General unit administration, attend bed meeting
1001–1100	Complete 5S audits, resolve open issues immediately
1101–1200	Cover for RNs during lunch rotation
1201–1300	Lunch, review e-mail and urgent messages
1301–1400	Review visuals, assign one task for improvement, record any abnormal conditions on frequency chart
1401–1500	General unit administration, review patients charts exceeding target length of stay
1501–1600	Department walkthrough with manager, Review visuals, update on status of action items
1601–1700	Cover for RNs during afternoon break rotation, meet with physicians on any urgent patient matters
1701–1800	Prepare for shift handover, address potential staffing concerns
1801–1900	5S check and handover to incoming charge nurse

Figure 5.6 Charge nurse standard work.

attention to the process—not only the results. In monitoring the process, we sustain improvements and provide consistent time and energy to resolving issues that arise. This consistent approach focusing on process is one of the key behaviors necessary to sustain improvement.

Some of you may think, "There is no way we can do this in our organization. We are too busy and the system is so unpredictable we cannot plan our day; we can only react to the circumstances we face each day." I can assure you that if you do not allocate time to review the visual management systems and also allocate time specifically for improvement, you will *not likely sustain* your improvement efforts over time. Management standard work bridges team improvements and long term success.

According to Mike de Graauw, a Lean Sensei and the president of Essential Consulting, you need "persistency, consistency, and tenacity" to manage in a

Lean environment. Mike's saying has become famous as a way to promote the right behaviors to sustain improvement. Persistency implies that you make a continued effort to root out and eliminate waste, never settling for the status quo. Consistency reminds us to never walk past an abnormal condition. Anything out of place in our 5S system, any deviation from standard work, and any item missing on the process control system must be addressed in real time *every time*. Tenacity means exercising diligence and stubbornness as we eliminate waste. Overcome obstacles and find a way to be successful…no matter what!

Managing process control is the first line of defense in keeping waste out of the system. If process control is designed well, you will see an abnormal condition at a glance. The steps you take as a manager to return the system to normal will be the keys to sustaining improvement.

Results Management

Managing your results is the final element of sustaining improvement. We can have a high performing (5S) workplace and effectively use process control to keep the waste out, but at the end of the day we are evaluated on results. We expect results in all five improvement dimensions (staff morale, quality, access or delivery, cost or productivity, and growth) and need a system to manage results visually. In Lean improvement, the tool for managing results is known as an MQDCG board. The letters represent the five improvement dimensions (morale, quality, delivery, cost, growth). Figure 5.7 is a standard results board set-up.

The columns across the top align with the improvement dimensions. The rows consist of a monthly trend chart, a daily trend chart, a frequency chart, and a corrective action plan. Results from the previous day are tabulated and placed on the daily trend chart. At the end of the month, the results are accumulated and listed on the monthly trend chart. The daily and monthly trend charts must have goal lines that enable us to see "actual versus planned" results (normal from abnormal) at a glance. If we miss the planned target for a day, we capture the key sources of variation on the frequency chart. The main sources of variation require improvement actions to close the gap and are listed in the corrective action column.

Typically, staff members calculate the daily totals and complete this chart and the frequency chart. Management is responsible for accumulating the totals for the monthly trend chart and assigning the corrective actions on the action plan. Best-run organizations meet briefly with each shift every day to review the status of the results board. This is often difficult to accomplish in healthcare where staff are dispersed throughout chaotic work environments like emergency departments and operating rooms. I offer a couple of tips to help these meetings happen.

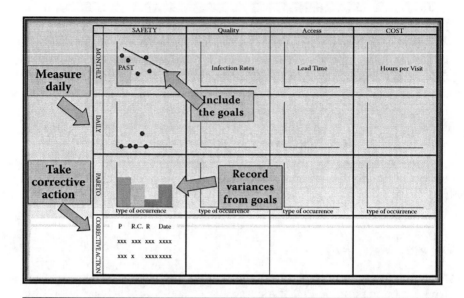

Figure 5.7   Results board.

- Hold meetings at a consistent time for each shift. The time you choose is not important; meeting each day with each shift is.
- Limit meeting time to 5 minutes. The agenda allows 1 minute to discuss each improvement dimension and assign correction actions to the team. Use a timer to end meetings after 5 minutes. It will be difficult to cover the whole agenda at first, but with practice you can achieve it regularly.
- The meetings are for *all* inter-professional staff and physicians. There will be days when not everyone can attend, but the meeting is *not optional.* It provides one chance during each shift to keep everyone informed on goals, targets, and actions. The staff cannot help you improve if they do not have access to and understand the requirements.
- Hold meetings in front of the results board. Seating is not needed. The meetings are designed to cover information on the board.
- Populate the graphs before meetings. Do not waste team time while graphs and charts are updated. (I actually prefer that the staff update the information because their work processes create the data.)

We must remain diligent to ensure that the activities we undertake will move our key measures. As stated earlier, sooner or later (and likely sooner), someone will ask about the organization's return on the Lean investment. When you have real-time data available, everyone understands why targets are met or missed. A detailed action plan gives you a complete results management system that will enable the entire team to help improve the key measures.

In this section, we focused on sustaining improvement and managing visually. We must sustain the improvements achieved by our team. The best way is by leveraging visual management in three areas: a robust 5S system, process control of standard work, and results management.

Support Improvement with Lean Training and Coaching

The more the world learns about Lean improvement, the more we understand what we don't know. And there is a *whole* lot we don't know. As you remove waste from your operations, wastes you didn't know you had will emerge. They will be more difficult to remove and may require more sophisticated tools. Great Lean organizations constantly augment their improvements with ongoing training and coaching. Let's review the concepts of Lean training and coaching.

If you were going to undertake scuba diving, would you read a few articles online, attend a few seminars, and go dive? Not likely. You would probably begin by finding an expert and asking many questions. You might find people who have diving experience and pick their brains as well. If you are still interested, you would enroll in a certification class, complete the course work, pursue pool training, and eventually complete open water dives.

If you want to be great at improvement, you might consider a similar track: find an expert, talk to others who walked the road earlier, and obtain extensive coaching. Lean sensei who have mastered Lean improvement are available and can guide you and your organization through the improvement processes. Having a Lean sensei teach improvement tools and approaches to your organization, train, minimize your risk, coach senior leadership, assist you with change management, and keep you focused on your journey is a step you should not skip. To find a Lean sensei, contact another organization (within or outside healthcare) and ask for a recommendation. To differentiate a Lean expert from a sensei, ask, "In how many industries have you provided Lean expertise?" Virtually every world-class organization has used senseis for 20 years or more. Their goal is not to go on their own, but rather use the experience of a master to strengthen the journey and continually challenge their approaches to improvement. The coaching aspects of Lean are multifaceted. Among the dozens of areas of specialization for Lean coaching, several are particularly effective for getting started. The key areas requiring coaching in your first year are covered in Table 5.3. Other coaching areas are:

Table 5.3 Sample Year One Coaching Topics

Coaching Activity	Description
Infrastructure coaching	Helps define resources for improvement including internal facilitators, improvement governance, and measurement tracking
Gemba walking	Learning model based on master/apprentice approach; involves walking the work area to review visual management system and management actions to support improvement
Management coaching	Supports line, middle, and senior management in learning to manage in a constantly improving environment
Managing for daily improvement (MDI)	Teaches operation to stabilize 4Ms (manpower, methods, mother nature/environment, and materials) for daily improvement
Problem solving	Blends cause-and-effect diagrams and 5 Whys to teach real-time problem solving
Visual management	Coaching to manage 5S, process control, and results; can cascade to include program-level improvement and enterprise-wide improvement
Kamishibai	Uses series of cascading audits to teach organization to live Lean culture
Management development	Coaching fundamentals of management such as setting and maintaining standards, improving standards, and developing people

- Kaizen preparation standard work
- Kaizen follow-up standard work
- Sustaining skills
- Measurement capture and reporting
- Cascading leadership standard work and leadership rounds
- Dealing with difficult employees
- Steering committee and governance terms of reference and standard meeting agenda
- Senior leadership coaching
- Project planning and improvement sequencing
- Physician engagement strategy

Table 5.4   Advanced Lean Tools

Tool	Description
Vertical value stream	Lean approach to world class project management; used in construction, IT deployment, Lean improvement, and wherever a project plan is needed and used.
3P	Production process preparation; new product or process development technique that invents new capability
2P	Process preparation; new product or process development technique that delivers new capability using existing technology
Heijunka	May not be considered advanced; may be introductory approach; levels work volume or mix to prevent batching and enable single item flow
Hoshin kanri	Used to deploy strategic plan; powerful senior leadership approach to aligning strategy horizontally and vertically across organization to deliver sustainable results; monitors process and outcomes of strategy to deliver world class rates of improvement
Statistical process control	Used to eliminate variability from a process; should be introduced when defects per million rate is approached
Kanban	Lean supply chain management system

- Communication strategy
- Board engagement strategy

As your journey continues, you will begin to identify new and exciting opportunities to see and eliminate waste. The improvement concepts of flow, pull, defect-free, and visual management offer hundreds of tools and improvement techniques you can use. The good news is that because many organizations have used Lean for decades, the advanced tools needed already exist. The bad news is that the hundreds of tools to choose from make tool selection difficult and it takes time to learn the techniques. As your organization progresses with the fundamental tools of improvement, you will soon be ready for more advanced approaches to eliminating waste. Some of these tools are listed in Table 5.4.

In addition to expanding knowledge in new tools and approaches, the staff and medical leadership at your hospital will need ongoing training to understand Lean. Everyone will need to be grounded in the five principles of improvement, the seven wastes, and A3 thinking. Over time, we expect everyone to become competent in the common tools for seeing and eliminating waste, and in the team-based improvement techniques of value stream mapping and analysis and kaizen improvement.

While learning by doing is encouraged, training of this breadth and depth will eventually require a more formal plan. World class organizations begin by educating the senior leadership and then having this team train the organization. Since it is very difficult to master all of the tools, expertise is usually divided across the leadership team. For example, one leader will become the expert on flow, another on pull. One person will become the internal expert on 5S and another on visual management. Over time, the responsibilities can be rotated so each member of the team can continue his or her personal development and master expertise in many areas. A great Lean improvement system supports ongoing coaching and training. Continuous improvement takes a lifetime to learn, so you will want to have training and coaching plans in place from the start.

Spread Improvement

If you have made and sustained improvement in one or more value streams and are now augmenting your improvement with the needed coaching and training to further develop your improvement skills, you are ready to "spread" your improvements, that is, extend them into additional areas. All organizations want to accelerate their rates of improvement. My general rule is that you can go as fast as you can sustain. Taking improvement across the organization should follow a calculated approach and the pace of spreading improvement should be based on meeting criteria (goals or milestones) *not* meeting time targets in a plan. Spreading (sharing) improvements involves two different approaches. In one approach, we move artifacts, products, or solutions developed in one area to another area. For example, maybe we have developed a great way to manage glucose testing on an inpatient unit. It may be so effective that other departments want to replicate it.

However, another type of spread means increasing the breadths of value streams being improved by an organization. New areas are introduced to Lean improvement for the first time. For example, assume we began our improvement in the laboratory and in an endocrinology clinic. Both areas completed their value stream mapping and analysis sessions and have begun to deliver improvement, establishing standard work and visual management. The results have been sustained and the organization now wants to add additional value streams for improvement. Perhaps we want to venture into the cardiac catheterization lab and emergency services, starting as always with value stream mapping and analysis sessions and continuing the improvement process accordingly. These

Table 5.5   Spread Approaches

Spread Approach	Advantages	Considerations
Replication of tools, process, and artifacts	Leverages tested solutions Key training points defined Solutions based on lean principles Rapid approach Design resources not consumed	Usually replicates product, not thinking Less buy-in to someone else's solutions Limits new ideas and innovation Difficult in not-invented-here environments Project management resources needed to manage change
Introducing additional value streams	Buy-in from start as current conditions and future conditions are developed and agreed upon and action plans are generated Engages many more team members in improvement New innovation with each opportunity Tailored improvement plans for each value stream	May be more resource-intensive than replication approach May take longer than replication approach Requires more infrastructure (skilled facilitators) within organization

two approaches to spread require different strategies. Before we talk about the strategies, we should differentiate the two approaches. Table 5.5 evaluates the two alternatives.

Most organizations are not faced with choosing one approach or the other because both approaches will be used to spread the improvements. We will review them in detail.

Replication of Artifacts, Products, Solutions, and Process

This approach is used when we want to adopt a solution from one area to another in its exact form (or in a form very close to the original). Perhaps you have

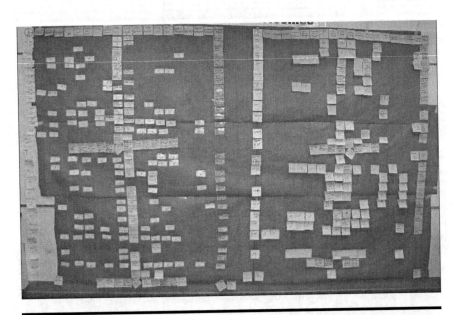

Figure 5.8 Vertical value stream example. (From CREMS, Central CCAC 2009. With permission.)

piloted a new standard process for cleaning a room on one unit and now want to take that process hospital-wide. To successfully achieve this replication, you will want to use a project management-based technique. Lean organizations use a tool known as a vertical value stream to manage projects. A vertical value steam is like a vertical Gantt chart. Using such a system, the project moves through several phases and passes clearly defined "tollgates" before moving to the next phase. An example of a vertical value stream is shown in Figure 5.8. The following steps illustrate how you can use vertical value stream mapping to spread your solutions.

1. Identify a representative sample of the key stakeholders affected by the change.
2. Thoroughly review the known solutions so the entire team understands the process, tools, and visual management systems.
3. Assign an end date for the project.
4. Develop criteria for passing each milestone. Criteria are measurable outcomes of process and/or results that must be met before moving to the next phase of a project. Table 5.6 shows typical spread plan tollgates and criteria.
5. Determine the tasks needed to pass the tollgate.

Table 5.6 Spread Plan Tollgates and Criteria

Tollgate	Criteria
Readiness for training	Materials and equipment purchased; visual management system mounted on wall; IT upgrades achieved
Readiness for launch	95% of staff trained in standard work; process control and results tracking systems in place; leadership rounds scheduled
Project closeout	95% adherence to standard work; deviations captured; results meeting target for 60 days

6. Assign accountability for the tasks to meet tollgate criteria.
7. Execute the tasks needed to meet the tollgate.
8. Hold a formal review to confirm that the tollgate criteria have been met before beginning the next phase of the project plan.
9. Capture lessons learned from the tollgate reviews to improve the organizational knowledge.
10. Repeat Steps 8 and 9 until the project is completed.

If you ensure you have met the tollgate criteria before you move to the next phase of the project plan, you will minimize rework later in the project. If you plan all the tasks necessary to meet the tollgate criteria, you minimize the number of steps needed to complete the project. The combined impact of these two design elements in your project plan can reduce the timeline for execution by 50 to 75%, while ensuring high quality results at the end of the project.

Adding Additional Value Streams

Throughout this chapter, we focused on delivering value stream improvement. In Step 2 of our roadmap for getting started, we discussed selecting and mapping value streams. If we retained the notes we made during value stream selection, we will find it simple to determine which value stream to select now. Using the Figure 5.1 chart, assume we still are trying to improve staff satisfaction. The graph shows we started in the value stream of emergency services. If we were going to add another value stream, which one would we select next? The chart indicates that adult medicine would be the next candidate. A word of warning: it will be *very tempting* to deviate from the data and embark on value stream mapping in an area of "high pain" for the organization. However, we must remain strategic in our deployment of Lean and stay focused on the areas that best help us meet our strategic outcomes. At times the area of pain will impact your outcome measures, but often it will not—and if it doesn't, beware! You have an obligation to direct your critical few improvement resources on the most strategic areas. Many organizations struggle because they undergo a lot of Lean improvement, but not all of it is strategic, and therefore it does not produce meaningful results. Finally, I'd like to offer a few other key points on adding value streams in your organization.

1. There is a limit to the number of value streams in which your organization can engage at any one time. This threshold is based on several criteria including organizational headcount, infrastructure (improvement resources), and your ability to sustain improvement. Add a value stream only when you have sustained improvement in an earlier one.

2. Consider administrative value streams as well as clinical value streams. While our business is healthcare delivery, the clinical teams can only absorb so much change. I have found that a ratio of 75% clinical value stream improvement to 25% administrative value stream improvement works well. Administrative value streams such as recruiting and on-boarding, supply chain management, and health records management (for example) can impact the pace of change within clinical value streams. Do not let clinical improvement get too far ahead of administrative improvement.

3. Don't exclude any areas of your business from the value stream selection process. Lean tools exist to deploy IT, perform help desk and call center operations, execute strategic planning and strategy deployment, create a new service, or design a room, clinic, unit, or entire facility. Lean ways can be applied effectively to parking, volunteer, and security services. One way to expand the breadth of Lean improvement is to use Lean in areas that may appear not applicable (to a novice). How about improving centralized scheduling and staffing, developing and implementing an evidence-based care map, improving foundation services (ending waste in fundraising), and shortening the cycle for clinical research? Hopefully you are getting the picture: a Lean approach applies anywhere work is done.

As you spread your improvements and increase your improvement pace, you are on your way to becoming a Lean organization! The improvement of multiple areas of an organization at the same time will help you achieve your measurable outcomes. In summary, the following steps will start your improvement:

1. Determine measurable outcomes for the organization that help achieve your strategic vision.
2. Select and map key value streams.
3. Begin improvement.
4. Manage visually and sustain your improvement.
5. Support your team through ongoing coaching and training.
6. Spread your improvements through a combination of replicating lean solutions and increasing the number of value streams you implement.

Are you ready to start?

Chapter 6

Leadership Lessons Learned

We have covered a lot of material to this point. We discussed several reasons why improvement is needed in healthcare, examined the fundamentals of improvement, and learned several tools for identifying and eliminating waste. We covered the applications of improvement and the dramatic results achieved by teams in healthcare environments. Finally, we discussed how to start improvement in your organization. By now, I hope you see how a culture of continuous improvement using Lean approaches can help your organization.

As you get started, you should be aware that no transformational improvement approach is without risk. The financial investment in staff, medical personnel, and process can be steep, and your results are not guaranteed. Having walked this improvement road with hundreds of clients and thousands of teams in a variety of industries, I can tell you there are many valuable lessons to be learned. You can leverage this experience. I'd like to share some key lessons that may help you avoid the most common mistakes.

Without a doubt, leadership is the single most important success factor in creating a culture of improvement. But let's be clear: I said "leadership" not "management." Management means doing things well. Leadership means creating a vision, inspiring and developing people to be their best, and doing the right things. The first mistake organizations often make is delegating all the leadership of improvement to a staff department such as a quality group or a project management office. You may get an improved department using this approach, but you won't get a transformed organization. Successful, sustained Lean improvement must be *led* at the highest level of the organization—the senior leadership team. To be successful, improvement activities require a *minimum* of 25% of your senior leadership's time, talent, and focus. What exactly is required to lead change? This chapter contains a short list of the most important behaviors and activities required from your corporate leadership along with descriptions of the activities. Here is what your senior leadership team needs to do.

Participate

There is no better way to learn the tools, change management approaches, and essential questions than to participate in an improvement activity such as a value stream analysis or a kaizen event. By participate, I mean act as a fully functioning team member. Being present part of the time and then skipping out for meetings and phone calls is not sufficient. (Nor is remaining in the session and spending a large portion of time scrolling through your Blackberry!)

Roll up your sleeves. Lead by example. Learn to see waste by using the actual tools and then use the improvement principles to eliminate it. At the senior leadership level, a commitment of one full improvement week per year would be a great start and more is even better. And the entire leadership team needs to participate, including the CEO, vice presidents, COO, chief of staff, and CFO.

Walk the Value Streams

Regular leadership rounds also constitute another requirement. In Lean, they're also known as gemba walking (introduced in Chapter 3) or walking the value stream. Keep in mind that a Lean leader is first a coach and mentor. Fortunately, participating on the teams and learning the tools will make you a better mentor and coach. Walking the value stream shows support for the improvement process, while allowing you to challenge the team when performance is off or not sustained and to recognize the team when a job is well done. Pay attention to the visual management systems and the results boards. What is important to you is important to your team. When you show your team that you are interested in the visual management systems, they will take notice.

Commit Resources to Ensure Success

In addition to participating and showing commitment through involvement, leaders can also show support by committing the resources required to be successful. A successful improvement experience requires investment in three areas: facilitation, team resources and improvement supplies.

Facilitation

Many organizations underestimate how much time it takes to improve. However, the preparation, the improvement team activities, and subsequent sustaining activities all require some skilled facilitation—by full-time resources to be effective. My rule is that you need one full-time person for each value stream you are improving. This person can be a dedicated resource or a seconded resource, but he or she must have full time involvement.

The responsibilities of the improvement facilitator are summarized in Table 6.1.

The data collection activities and the suite of sustaining activities require extensive amounts of time. Part-time resources generally are ineffective in handling both sets of activities well. Ineffective data collection leads to less-than-optimal results. Ineffective sustaining activities may produce slow results or even project failure.

Table 6.1 Improvement Facilitator Core Responsibilities

Responsibilities	
Become internal Lean improvement expert	Train staff and medical personnel on Lean principles, practices, and process
Monitor preparation activities	Facilitate improvement activities
Assist in sustaining activities	Develop line management
Teach visual management to organization	Assist in managing breadth and depth of improvement
Coordinate logistics for improvement	Assist in population of improvement scorecard
Develop additional team leaders	Assist in development of visual management systems
Assist in managing improvement plan at value stream and corporate levels	Capture data or assist in its capture

Team Resources

In addition to leadership facilitation, you will need to invest in team resources. Recall that Lean is a process of people and everyone must participate. Implementing a team to work through an A3 or a kaizen event means that team resources must be available. Having the right team working on the right project with the right targets is a fundamental requirement for success. You should plan to allow staff and medical personnel to be available to work on improvement.

An improvement team usually consists of six to ten people to ensure that all key stakeholders are involved. Additionally, you need to give middle management some "wiggle room" to improve. They must have some dedicated time to focus on change management and build a Lean culture. You should evaluate the priorities of your middle management. Are they focused on small projects that are less important to their departments than improvement? Good leaders keep those directly reporting to them focused on the right things. De-emphasizing the least important activities can go a long way toward ensuring success.

Improvement Supplies

Finally, you will want to allocate some resources to cover the supplies and materials needed for an improvement effort. Office supplies are necessary for improvement activities. To start, make sure you have these supplies on hand:

Supply of 3 × 3-inch sticky notes in multiple colors
Scissors
Roll of 36- or 48-inch wide butcher paper
Roll of 1-inch masking tape (or other method to attach paper to walls)
Roll of ¾-inch clear adhesive tape
Two pads of flip chart paper and easels
Pack of fine point black markers
Set of multicolored flip chart markers
Several solar calculators
Several clipboards
Several stopwatches

Other supplies are needed for the visual management systems. Floor tape and label making equipment are needed for 5S training. Dry erase boards (3 × 4 feet or larger) are needed for process control systems. They can be acquired on demand so there is no need to purchase them in advance. However, you should plan ahead by establishing a small budget to cover the cost of these supplies. Do not under estimate this step. I have seen teams "spin" for three days because no one in management knew who was going to pay for a $20 chart rack.

External Resources

It is also important to consider a resource that provides improvement expertise. Just as you would consult an accountant to help with your taxes or a personal trainer to help you get in shape, consider hiring a Lean expert to help you with improvement. Engaging outside expertise to help with training, leadership development, infrastructure development, and team improvement is a wise investment for many organizations.

External Lean expertise comes in many forms, from a Lean expert with expertise in one field, to a Lean sensei who has skills in many business areas. A good external resource will shorten your lead time for results, accelerate the breadth and depth of your improvement, minimize your organizational risk, and assist in development of management and leadership. Additionally, an outside resource is not tied to your political and organizational structures. This is a tremendous asset because an outside source has an impartial ability to focus on process instead of designing an improvement system based on personalities.

One piece of advice is critical when you consider outside expertise. Seek experts who have practical experience in management development. The Lean tools, while potentially overwhelming at first, are the easiest areas involved in improvement. The most difficult aspect is changing the way management thinks, acts, and behaves. You will see a wide variation in Lean expert capability when you move beyond tools and into management and leadership development.

By providing the appropriate resources for improvement including facilitation resources, team member participation, "wiggle room" (dedicated time and flexibility) for middle management, and a small budget for improvement supplies, you will enhance your chances for success. Additional benefits can be gained by the use of outside Lean expertise, particularly with respect to Lean management development.

Hold People Accountable

A successful Lean implementation requires accountability. In many organizations, a healthcare team consists of a collection of individual contributors working at their own paces and achieving different outcomes. A great Lean system begins by creating team-based standard work and then making sure that everyone consistently follows that standard. Ideally, we want all individuals involved to follow the standard because they believe in the standard and are committed to the new process. That is not usually the place to begin. Inevitably 85% of the people will follow the standard, but the other 15% will require "encouragement."

The "frozen middle" is a term often used in Lean circles to refer to middle management. The front line staff generally is excited about participating in the change process and presenting their ideas. This group usually proposes ideas that are embraced and implemented quickly. Senior leadership is generally pleased with Lean improvement because it brings about a sense of excitement in the organization and delivers meaningful results in a short time.

Middle management is caught between the two prongs of the change process. In a Lean environment, all existing management systems and personality-based processes are eliminated. This is often threatening to the middle managers who have not yet developed their new management systems and do not yet trust Lean tools and approaches. Additionally, after visual management systems are in place, a manager's operation is completely transparent for everyone. Many managers are not comfortable with this visibility.

As a middle manager, I was responsible for work assignments, scheduling, documentation, process work flows, managing budgets, and much more. In a Lean environment, many of the systems and tools used in management are replaced by new Lean processes, standard work, and visual management systems. When the old systems are dismantled, managers feel very uncomfortable. What happens—often unintentionally—is that managers tend to hold on to the old systems and tools. This behavior is counterproductive in an improving environment.

It is essential to be very supportive of middle management during the change, to help it let go of the old systems as quickly as possible, and embrace the new methods. Leadership needs to provide middle management with training on the new system and middle management must be held accountable for the both the process and the results. Just as we expect the staff to follow standard work, we expect management to follow the Lean management processes. These processes are management's standard work.

We also expect healthcare organizations to hold physicians accountable. While physicians certainly have much more autonomy than the rest of the staff, they should also follow certain standards as well. These include (as a very small sample) compliance with start and stop times, meeting standards for the quality of paperwork and documentation, adherence to evidence-based best practices, and consistent adherence to infection prevention and control practices. I have seen many improvement efforts fail because the organization and the medical leadership did not hold the medical staff accountable for following the standard work. We'll discuss physicians more in the next key lesson.

One last thought on accountability. While we prefer the improvement experience to be positive for patients, medical practitioners, and staff, it may be a difficult or even unpleasant experience. Sometimes improving means changing work hours or moving work from one resource to another. Sometimes improvement requires people to do tasks they don't like in the best interests of patients. As leaders, we must always do the right thing in service of the patient.

On rare occasions, staff may decide they do not want to follow the new process. It is your job as a manager to inspire your staff to follow the standard work. On even rarer occasions, an individual will need to be disciplined for not following the new process. While I do not want to anticipate the need for disciplinary action, I would be remiss if I did not acknowledge this likelihood. As I tell managers, "There's a reason you're a manager." One of those reasons is your requirement to hold staff accountable to standards. To summarize this important point: if you are not going to have a culture of accountability, then you can stop with Lean or any other type of improvement for that matter. You have no chance for success if the administrative staff, medical staff, and management do not consistently follow standard work. Remember: no standard, no improvement!

Engage Physicians

Healthcare systems engage many different professionals: nurses, physicians, respiratory therapists, occupational therapists, and physiotherapists, along with social workers, pharmacists, laboratory technicians, and imaging technologists. With all of these professional people engaged in healthcare, why are we singling out physicians?

Physicians are in the unique position of being able to choose whether to follow organizational standards. Physicians can deviate from standard order sets and clinical pathways, add or subtract diagnostics, change medication regimens, and decide when to discharge. No other staff function in the healthcare environment has this unique autonomy.

Is this a bad thing? Absolutely not! However, it is essential to engage physicians in improvement work to a far greater extent than popping into a room on occasion during an improvement activity. What we desire is a healthcare system that is physician led! Who is in a better position to lead improvement than medical staff? Clinical healthcare needs physician champions. We need to synthesize the continuous improvements in practice, therapeutics, medicines, surgical procedures, and diagnostics to deliver (and even invent) better evidence-based, best-practice care.

On many occasions, I have seen an inter-professional team collaborate with a physician to develop an evidence-based clinical pathway utilizing the latest technology, protocols, order sets, and treatments. After a team reaches alignment in both process and format, the pathway is documented in a manner consistent with the requirements of health medical records. The work is piloted on a few patients with favorable results in outcomes.

When presented to the physicians working in the department, what do you think the reception is? Typically, the pathway is received with skepticism, criticism, and an offer to make many changes. Rarely is the pathway adopted and followed. The question is why?

In my view, the reason is that physicians were not sufficiently invested in the change at the beginning of the process. The behavior of rejecting change is not specific to physicians. In any area of professional specialization, change is always easier to accept when you are invested in and part of the change. This behavior becomes an opportunity for Lean organizations. Rather than "managing around" physicians, how do we inspire and engage them to lead quality improvement?

Great organizations have a strategy to engage physicians. This strategy may include creating a value proposition specifically for physicians (explaining the value of engaging in administrative improvement work, for example), holding special training and education sessions, leveraging the medical leadership, and in some cases providing funding to allow for full participation. Experienced Lean organizations even build improvement requirements for physicians into their physician agreements. I encourage you to engage the physician group early in the Lean improvement process so that you can build this strategy collaboratively.

As you build your engagement strategy, a few areas of focus are summarized in Table 6.2. The best Lean healthcare organizations have great physician engagement, but no organization starts with high levels of engagement. Trust is built one physician at a time, one team at a time, and one department at a time. When physicians participate in the improvement work, most enjoy the experience and many will be repeat improvers. The key is establishing momentum quickly with your physicians and then maintaining their engagement through the improvement process.

Establish Governance Structure

When you see some results from your first value stream, you will start getting requests from many areas of the organization to help them improve. And you should! After all, everyone has a need to improve quality, improve access, and lower costs while creating an inspired staff. Your organization may also be asking about speed, scope, and results. How fast should they improve? How many resources are needed? Are you getting a return on your investment? These questions are best answered by establishing a guiding coalition or a Lean steering committee that has several key responsibilities in guiding your organization through the change process. The committee must:

Table 6.2 Beginning Physician Engagement

Opportunity	Key Points
Standardize quality	Beginning here drives the most waste from healthcare. It allows development of department standards to improve outcomes and reduce costs for materials, supplies, diagnostics, and medicine. Use evidence-based approaches and agree on standards as a department. Physicians must agree as a team. Individual preference drives a lot of waste and variability even if each physician uses his or her own evidence-based approach.
Standardize process	Create department-wide process standards for physicians (e.g., where to keep patient charts, where to store gloves). Start with easy items and progress to more complicated areas. Physicians must hold each other accountable for following standards. This begins with department chiefs who should model appropriate behaviors.
Follow Lean principles and approaches when applying solutions	Use creativity before capital. Technology is a consideration but should be selected following standardization of process. Refrain from jumping to IT as the initial solution. Solutions should be patient- (not provider-) focused; use of improvement principles should eliminate waste. Use A3 thinking. Refrain from jumping to solutions before understanding the problems. Solutions should never be personality based.

- Establish measurement systems and targets for monitoring success.
- Ensure that the results are captured.
- Select areas of focus (value streams) for the organization.
- Provide oversight to ensure development of staff, medical staff, and management via training and hands-on activity.
- Remove organizational barriers (organizational structures, systems, people, policies and procedures, compensation programs, promotion policies, etc.).
- Monitor the pace of change. If you move too slowly, you lose momentum; if you move too quickly, sustainability of the program will suffer.

Many organizations do not want to set up yet another steering committee. Perhaps they feel that too many committees exist across healthcare organizations already.

They prefer to add the Lean activity to the strategy council, operations committee, or quality council. I do *not* recommend this practice. Lean improvement will require enough activity to warrant a dedicated committee's full attention. Remember that Lean is *not* a project; it is a management system of continuous improvement that results in a transformation of your organizational culture.

The steering committee should meet monthly for 90 to 120 minutes. It should consist of 8 to 12 people. Figure 6.1 presents a sample Lean steering committee. Standard meeting rules should be followed. A timekeeper should be designated and someone should be assigned to record meeting minutes. Minutes from the previous meeting should be approved. A standard agenda should be followed. Figure 6.2 is a sample meeting agenda.

During the meeting, action items are assigned and the team members are expected to complete their assignments before the next meeting. Accountability for completing assignments is a prerequisite of effective meetings. This group will provide oversight for the overall Lean improvement journey for your organization. To underscore the importance of participation (discussed earlier in this chapter), I find that the members of this committee are better team members after they participate on an improvement team.

Position	Function
Chair	CEO
Co- Chair	Operations Executive for your organization
Team Members	Chief of Medical Staff
	CFO
	Representative from Marketing/Communications
	Representative from Human Resources
	Leader of your lean program (often this is the Director of Quality)
	Corporate leader for quality, patient safety and risk management
	1 to 4 other teams members as needed. (These members do not all have to be leadership and can include administrative and medical staff)

Figure 6.1 Sample Lean steering committee.

Time	Agenda Item	Lead
1300	Check In and Welcome	Chair
1305	Review Previous Minutes	Chair
1310	Value Stream #1 Results to date Countermeasures to close the gaps Action Plans Upcoming Events	Value Stream Leader #1
1325	Value Stream #2 Results to date Countermeasures to close the gaps Action Plans Upcoming Events	Value Stream Leader #2
1340	Value Stream #3 Results to date Countermeasures to close the gaps Action Plans Upcoming Events	Value Stream Leader #3
1350	Corporate Roll Up of results — review scorecard	CFO
1400	Review Integrated LEAN improvement schedule for next 3 months	Lean Leader
1410	Developing People Review Engagement Statistics	Lean Leader
1420	Are there any corporate barriers that need to be removed?	Co-Chair
1430	Adjourn	All

Figure 6.2 Sample meeting agenda.

Address Antibodies

One of the challenges you will face as an organization is how to deal with people who want no part of the change process. These people may be overt resisters; they may be extremely vocal about their displeasure or they may be passively opposed to change and simply uncooperative. These people can come from any part of your organization: staff, physicians, managers, directors, and even members of the senior leadership team. Experience shows that 5 to 20% of an organization will resist change. This is not an insignificant number and you must deal quickly and effectively with this population or you may fail to change the culture.

Lean organizations call these resisters of change "antibodies." Let me explain the analogy. When an infection invades the human body, antibodies become active to preserve the status quo. The antibodies have a specific purpose: return the human system to its normal state. The same principle applies when you try to change the culture of an organization. When change is infused into your organization, the antibodies will activate to preserve your existing culture.

Is this a bad thing? The answer is yes, but with a small explanation. Not every antibody has ill intentions. Some antibodies become active from concern that the changes will be harmful to the organization. Unfortunately, antibodies multiply. If you do not address the antibodies when they first appear, they will influence other people. Left unchecked, this group can totally derail the change process and end your attempt to create a culture of continuous improvement.

The question is, "How do we deal with the antibodies?" The first line of defense is to make expectations very clear when you begin improving. Leadership must have a crystal clear understanding of the reasons for change, what is expected from all participants, who will be affected, and the consequences for those who choose not to participate. This message, called an "elevator speech," must be tailored for the different levels of the organization. It is usually prepared for administrative staff, medical staff, and management and should be delivered very early in the change process.

The next way to address antibodies is to involve them in the change process because most people are much more likely to accept their own ideas than someone else's! Most (80%) of your antibodies will completely change their positions after they participate in a kaizen event or an A3 improvement project and the change may be very dramatic. On countless occasions, I have seen a staff associate formerly labeled a troublemaker become a great Lean champion following an opportunity to participate in improvement. Turning someone considered difficult into a believer and practitioner of continuous improvement is a great win for your organization!

On rare occasions, participation is not sufficient to turn an antibody. In these cases, you will need to apply situational leadership, dealing with the staff associate on a case-by-case basis. The organization must address antibodies consistently. You cannot follow different standards for different layers or departments within your organization. In Lean circles, you commonly hear that "the fastest way to change the people is to change the people." This may require you to separate an individual from your organization who not only fails to participate in improvement, but also fails to follow standard work and negatively influences others. This may not be a frequent occurrence but it does happen at all levels of organizations.

In summary, antibodies become active to preserve the status quo of your organizational culture. We need to address them quickly to prevent negative influences on other staff members. The best way to address antibodies is through clear communication and by getting them involved.

Develop and Deliver Communication Strategy

We discussed the importance of communication in addressing antibodies. One of the reasons for failure of change efforts is that they do not create enough momentum to influence enough people to get to the "tipping point" of change. The best way to influence people is to get them involved; however, we cannot start improving everywhere at the same time. We must reach all parts of the organization simultaneously through an effective communication campaign. In particular, we must influence the areas we are focused on improving. At a minimum, we need an effective communication system to let affected areas know about the changes taking place now and the ones that are pending. Lean organizations address the communication gap with a strong communication strategy.

In our communication strategy, we want to reach as many people as possible. For the broader organization, I suggest you begin by communicating the reason for change. Identify and communicate why it is essential for your organization to improve. Depending on current performance, this message can vary significantly. The initial communication can address the following questions:

What is our burning platform to improve?
What have we done in the past to improve?
What successes and learning have occurred?
Why are we choosing Lean as an improvement strategy?
How is Lean different from other improvement approaches?
Who is affected?
What is expected of those affected?
What's in it for me?
What if I don't want to participate?
How will this change impact other parts of the organization?
How were the initial areas of focus chosen?
What are the results anticipated?
Will there be lay-offs following the changes?

This detailed communication sets the tone for the upcoming changes. Any questions that you anticipate should be addressed. Remember, administrative and medical staff will devise their own answers to any questions you fail to address. Their made-up questions and corresponding answers can start rumors that may later require many hours of damage control to address.

After you start improving, you should implement recurring methods of communication to keep the organization informed about progress, activities, and results. These regular communication vehicles may include (but are not limited to) a Lean newsletter, webinars, information posted on bulletin boards, website or intranet updates, town hall meetings, and staff and department meetings. Great organizations use multiple forms of communication to keep their staffs and medical personnel informed.

Redeployment versus Unemployment

The focus of Lean is to create a culture of improvement. To foster this culture, we must create an environment in which the administrative staff, medical staff, and management trust the organization. Job security is a key area of trust. As wasteful activity is eliminated, personnel resources are freed up. If there is no meaningful work for these resources, it can be tempting to downsize the organization through lay-offs, particularly if the financial position of the organization is not strong.

The fastest way to destroy your continuous process improvement journey is to lay off an employee following an improvement. In good faith, we bring administrative and medical staff together to eliminate waste from the organization. We simultaneously improve staff morale, patient quality, and safety; we increase access and lower costs. We cannot "reward" our staff for this effort by asking them to find jobs elsewhere. The first time you lay someone off as a result of an improvement, your chances for further improvement drop to *zero*. No one will improve himself out of a job. Why would he?

But let me add a caveat. Lean organizations meet staff needs by offering employment security, not job security. If we identify a need for 15 registration clerks following an improvement, and 19 registration clerks are currently on staff, what do we do with the surplus? Lean organizations use the *redeployment* term; they redeploy the four surplus staff members to open positions. Admittedly, those positions may require a shift change or other adaptation, but they allow the staff to be retained. Think redeployment not unemployment!

Why is redeployment essential? The answer is simple. By far, most organizational expenses relate to staffing. Let's reflect on that. Staff members certainly need salaries and benefits, but what are the other costs? Employees also need telephones, computers, parking spaces, personal lockers, and desks. They use materials and equipment, consume office supplies, and need break rooms, microwaves, and refrigerators. Many of these items represent ongoing operational expenses. Look at your budget, connect each line item to your staff, and you'll likely be amazed to discover how much of your budget goes to supporting your personnel.

As managers, we have a responsibility to use our resources wisely. If we can avoid adding resources by eliminating wasteful activity, we should take full advantage of that opportunity. Likewise, if we free up resources, we should make them available to the rest of the organization via a redeployment strategy. We can consider many alternatives to layoffs through a redeployment hierarchy that includes the following strategies:

- Reduce temporary or agency staff
- Implement a strategy for not replacing staff lost to attrition
- Reduce or eliminate overtime
- "Insource" services that are presently outsourced
- Add new services with the freed-up resources
- Run temporary improvement teams to accelerate improvement

On the other hand, it may be too late for you to avoid reducing headcount. Perhaps your financial position indicates that you have no choice. Can you still deploy a Lean management system? Absolutely, but you must address the personnel situation first. Any staffing changes should be finalized before you begin to improve. In this situation, the challenge you face is resourcing the improvement teams with a smaller staff. In some organizations this can be a difficult proposition. However, if we want to show respect for all people (a basic tenet of Lean), we must address staffing issues in a fair and up-front way. It is disrespectful to use continuous improvement as a reason to lay off staff.

You may be asking one additional question regarding redeployment: who should be redeployed? Should we redeploy the worst staff member or the best one, go by seniority, or leave the decision to the process owner? If you work in a unionized environment, the answer is straightforward. Any change in staffing must comply with the language of your collective bargaining agreement. For a non-union environment, I suggest a new paradigm. Great organizations always redeploy their best performers. This may come as a shock! Believe me, as a former manager, I devised all kinds of strategies to retain (actually to hoard) my best people. You may be asking (as I did), "Now you want me to give up my best employee willingly?"

Lean organizations celebrate redeployment as a tremendous organizational success. When we redeploy, we reward our best performers by giving them opportunities to learn new skills. We don't want to give such opportunities to just anyone. Our best and brightest should have opportunities to advance and develop. The remaining team will survive in our Lean organization. Throughout the Lean improvement that preceded the redeployment, you created a new process with standard work and visual management. As a result of standard work, *everyone* can improve performance. And visual management gives you control of both process and results. There will never be a better time to release your best performer for an exciting new opportunity.

Demand and Monitor Results

This leadership lesson is about expectations. When you satisfy your curiosity and participate on a team, you will quickly learn that 95% of the work done is non-value added activity. To achieve Lean, we want to eliminate and reduce non-value added activity. When you see this for yourself, your expectations of what is possible will change. Using Lean, you can *expect* double-digit improvement in performance. Remember we are trying to eliminate the non-value added activities that account for 95% of effort. A well run team should improve the key dimensions of staff morale, quality, access, and cost by more than 10%. If you are just beginning to improve, I expect that your results will be even better, because you will eliminate more waste. As a leader, you have the right to demand results using a Lean improvement system. Create a sense of urgency in the teams. Take in interest in the daily, weekly, and monthly performance.

Expect Improvement!

Don't be blind to your role. You will need to support the teams. Barriers will appear and antibodies will need to be addressed. Your organization will need a governance structure to be successful and it will have to engage and inspire physicians. A sound communication strategy is required to guide the organization through the *what* and *why* of change.

Finally, throughout all these improvement activities, never stop believing! You must demand and monitor results. If you do, your achievements will be significant. A Lean management system can take your organization where it's never been: a place where both staff and medical personnel are excited to come to work and patients get the world-class care they deserve—a place where access increases and essential healthcare services are offered to more people in your community every day and delivered in a cost-effective way, allowing your organization to maintain excellent fiscal health year after year.

Summary

As a leader in a healthcare organization, you know how essential your services are to the people you serve. Today, it's more important than ever that healthcare services be provided in an efficient, safe, and cost-effective way. Lives depend on our ability to run our organizations well. Without dedicated efforts at improvement, and a sound management system to help us get there, we put our communities at risk.

Fortunately, more and more healthcare organizations today are discovering the beauty of Lean: a management system of simple principles and methods that can be implemented in any organization to generate measurable, lasting results of improvement. You've taken the first step by simply reading this book. Now I encourage you to move forward with Lean in your organization. Inspire others and lead positive change. Watch how Lean thinking revitalizes your organization and sets the stage for great achievements. So much is possible when you apply the Lean approach to everything you do.

I think James Womack left the world with some powerful thoughts in his April 2010 Lean Enterprise Institute e-newsletter.* "No one who has tried to create a complete Lean enterprise, with the hands-on participation of top management, has failed to achieve dramatic results. And that is a very powerful statement.

"We are always looking for a crisis as our moment of opportunity and the world's healthcare systems are all now heading into deep crises as demographics, new technology, and a history of weak process management produces an unsustainable situation. This may be the single most important contribution of Lean thinking to society in this generation and we already have the knowledge to transform healthcare delivery systems. All we need to do is to act together to rapidly deploy our knowledge."

May God bless you on your journey.

---

* Womack, J. April 1, 2010. The end of the beginning. Lean Enterprise Institute e-newsletter. http://www.leanuk.org/downloads/jim/jim_eletter_201004.pdf

Glossary of Lean Terms

2P: Short form of *process preparation*; approach used to develop a new process or product. 2P begins with a voice of the customer activity, develops seven ways to operationalize each key task in the process, analyzes the seven ways using a Pugh analysis, and ends with the seven flows to define the new process.

5S: Five steps whose names begin with *S* that are used to develop a high performing work area. *Seiri* is removing unneeded or unwanted items (equipment, tools, supplies, materials, information) from the workplace. *Seiton* is the neat arrangement of remaining items: "a place for everything and everything in its place." *Seiso* is thorough cleaning of the workplace to return it to like-new condition. *Seiketsu* is the creation of standard conditions to keep the workplace standardized and organized by creating practices that enable standard work and proper work flow. *Shitsuke* is the personal discipline required to achieve the first four steps.

5S event: Team-based rapid cycle process used to implement the 5S steps in a work area while simultaneously training staff.

5 Whys: Approach used to identify the root cause of a problem and develop people. Beginning with the problem observed (direct cause), ask why the problem occurred and give an answer that directly addresses that question. Repeating the process five times will reveal the root cause.

7 quality tools: Seven common approaches to analysis often used in solving quality-related problems: cause-and-effect diagram, flowchart, check sheet, control chart, histogram, scatter diagram, and Pareto chart.

7 wastes: Forms of waste found in operations: overproduction, overprocessing, waiting, motion, transportation, inventory, and defects.

A3: Process and thinking for problem solving based on the scientific method; frequently used to document problem solving exercises, status reports, and business cases; named for the size of report paper.

Andon: Visual or audible signal that identifies an abnormal condition; typically combined with a stop-the-line mentality: a process is stopped when an abnormality occurs until the source of the abnormality can be detected and recurrence prevented.

Antibody: Person who resists change.

Batch: Approach by which large quantities of items (batches) are processed then moved to the next operation.

Cause and effect diagram: Graphic method used to develop possible causes of a known effect (problem). Key areas for brainstorming are developed around a standard set of categories, typically the 6Ms (manpower, measurement, methods, materials, mother nature, and machinery) or the 4Ps (people, process, policy, place); also known as a fishbone or Ishikawa diagram.

Communication circle: Tool used to show the waste of transactions and hand-offs of information.

Continuous improvement: Mindset adopted by organizations to repeatedly identify and eliminate waste.

Current state: Workflow of current operation; used for value stream mapping.

Cycle time: Time required to complete a process determined by direct observation.

Cycle time/takt time bar chart (Ct/Tt bar chart): Visual tool that displays how each staff person is loaded against the takt time. The chart shows the process takt time, the manual cycle time of each person in the process, and the minimum staffing calculation. Minimum staffing is equal to the sum of the cycle times divided by the takt time. The chart is used to highlight wasted manpower and bottlenecks and is a key to improving productivity; also known as a loading diagram.

Defect: Work that needs to be redone or examined; error that finds its way to the customer.

Direct observation: Best lean approach for identifying waste; involves going to an area and observing a process to identify waste; often combined with capturing time elements of a process to "quantify" waste.

Failure mode effects analysis: Quality tool used to identify key risk factors in a process and take action to mitigate the risk.

Flow: Processing a single unit of work through a series of steps in a continuous manner, at the rate of customer demand, in a standardized way. Ideally only value-added tasks are linked together.

Flow diagram: Lean tool used to document a process; diagram illustrates work flow and highlights process stops and starts, hand-offs, and disconnects.

Future state: Future workflow based on use of the lean design attributes of flow, pull, defect-free, and visual management; aspect of value stream mapping.

Gemba: Japanese term for "real place" used to describe the place where work is done.

Gemba walk: Management approach used to develop a subordinate. Following the master–apprentice model, the experienced leader walks through the work area with the subordinate to teach the subordinate how to identify waste and develop and evaluate plans for improvement. The mentor teaches the subordinate to practice kaizen (see and eliminate waste).

Genchi genbutsu: Japanese term for "go and see." To truly understand a situation, one must "go and see" the situation at the point where the work is done and the value is created.

Heijunka: Leveling of volume and mix of work over a fixed period; concept used to reduce batching while efficiently meeting customer demand.

Heijunka box: Tool used to level the mix and volume of work.

Hoshin kanri: Management approach to identifying key strategic goals and developing plans to realize these goals; concludes with monthly reviews of processes and outcomes; also known as hoshin planning or policy deployment.

Inventory: Materials and information that accumulate between process steps.

Kaizen: Process used for continuous improvement to eliminate waste and create more value.

Kaizen event: Team-based approach to rapid cycle improvement. Spanning 2–5 days, depending on the scope of the activity, the scientific method is followed to deliver an improved process in a portion of a value stream ending with standard work, visual management, and process control.

Kanban: Japanese term loosely translated to mean "signboard." Scheduling system based on the principle of pull used determine what, when, and how much to make.

Line balancing: Method used to equally divide work among work stations after waste has been eliminated. Ideally, each staff member will be loaded equally with a work amount equal to or slightly less than the takt time.

Loading diagram: *See* cycle time/takt time bar chart.

Mistake proofing: Work methods designed to prevent the person doing the work from making an error; also known as error proofing.

Motion: Operator movement in excess of that required to complete a task.

Non-value-added: Activity that consumes time, space, or resources but does not directly meet the needs of customers; also known as waste.

Overprocessing: Doing work related tasks in excess of value as defined by the customer.

Overproduction: Producing or doing more, sooner, or faster than required by the next step in the process.

Performance board: Tool that shows results of a process; differs from the process control board in that it details outcome results in lieu of process measures.

Plan, do, check, act (PDCA): Cycle of improvement based on scientific method; changing a process by implementing change, measuring the result, and taking action to standardize or stabilize the change.

Poka-yoke: Japanese term for mistake proofing; quality control method that designs a work process that cannot create a defect.

Process control: Visual management tool for discerning abnormal conditions in the output of a process. In the common design, the plan and the actual output and sources of variation are documented in real time.

Process control board: Tool that displays process control; shows plan and actual performance of a process.

Pugh analysis: Quantitative technique used to evaluate multiple options against a set of criteria.

Pull: Signal used to link areas of continuous flow together; method to control work by having downstream activities signal their upstream requirements; used to reduce or eliminate waste of overproduction.

Sensei: An experienced person who has mastered the Lean approaches to improvement and management.

Sequence of operations: Recipe for a process; step-by-step detail of standard work; represents one-third of the requirement of standard work.

Spaghetti map: Diagram demonstrating the path and distance of travel of an employee, supply, or machine; highlights the waste of motion and/or transportation.

Standard work: Work procedures that define how an operator will complete a task or process. Standard work is based on three elements: sequence of operations, takt time, and standard work in process.

Standard work combination sheet: Worksheet for documenting standard work; it documents the sequence of operations and the takt time and also shows manual task times, automatic task times, and walking times.

Standard work in process (SWIP): Amount of inventory needed to maintain continuous flow between two processes.

Steering committee: Body designated to govern lean improvement at the value stream or enterprise level of an organization.

Takt time: Theoretical calculation for determining the rhythm of output of a process in time units; calculation consists of dividing the available time to do work by the volume of work to be done.

Time observation: *See* direct observation.

Toyota Production System: Management system to achieve excellence by providing the highest possible quality, in the shortest time, at the lowest cost by removing wasted time and activity.

Transportation: Unnecessary movement of people, materials, or equipment; also known as waste of conveyance.

True north measure: Operational excellence comes from five key areas: staff morale (human development), quality, delivery (lead time), cost, and growth. A high level strategic measure of one of the five areas of operational excellence is a true north measure. Such measures serve as a compass for aligning effort and direction.

Value-added: Activity that directly meets the needs of a customer.

Value-added/non-value-added analysis: Technique for determining whether each task step adds or does not add value. Typically a value-added task is assigned a green dot and a non-value-added task receives a red dot. A typical process ratio is *no* non-value-added parts to one value-added part.

Value stream: Activities that deliver value to a customer.

Value stream mapping (VSM): Tool used to reveal waste in a value stream and develop a plan for improvement.

Vertical value stream map: Project planning approach designed to deliver the correct value to a customer while generating the least waste; begins by defining milestones followed by backward planning of tasks needed to meet the milestones, thus ensuring that most of the investment represents value added.

Visual management: System that reveals transparency of normal and abnormal conditions to allow identification of problems at a glance and immediate correction.

Waiting: Customer delays caused by the lack of supplies, equipment, information, and/or resources.

Waste: Activity that consumes time, space, and/or resources and fails to create value for customers.

Zero defects: Mindset based on the premise that while humans are prone to errors, the errors need not become defects by reaching customers. It is possible to achieve a zero-defect system.

Index